PRIVATE CONSULTING

Barbara L. Johnson has worked as a financial writer and editor for a number of San Francisco financial institutions and has been a private editorial consultant for seven years. She has written numerous articles and books, including *Book Scouting: How to Turn Your Love for Books Into Profit,* published by Prentice-Hall, Spectrum Books.

Prentice-Hall International, Inc., *London*
Prentice-Hall of Australia Pty. Limited, *Sydney*
Prentice-Hall Canada Inc., *Toronto*
Prentice-Hall of India Private Limited, *New Delhi*
Prentice-Hall of Japan, Inc., *Tokyo*
Prentice-Hall of Southeast Asia Pte. Ltd., *Singapore*
Whitehall Books Limited, *Wellington, New Zealand*

BARBARA L. JOHNSON

PRIVATE CONSULTING

HOW TO TURN EXPERIENCE INTO EMPLOYMENT DOLLARS

A SPECTRUM BOOK

Prentice-Hall, Inc., Englewood Cliffs, New Jersey 07632

Library of Congress Cataloging in Publication Data

Johnson, Barbara L.
    Private consulting.

    "A Spectrum Book."
    Includes index.
    1. Business consultants.   I. Title.
HG69.C6J63   1982   658.4'6   82-7688
ISBN 0-13-710889-3   AACR2
IBSN 0-13-710871-0 (pbk.)

This Spectrum Book can be made available to businesses
and organizations at a special discount when ordered in
large quantities. For more information, contact:
Prentice-Hall, Inc., General Publishing Division,
Special Sales, Englewood Cliffs, New Jersey 07632.

1 2 3 4 5 6 7 8 9 10

ISBN 0-13-710889-3

ISBN 0-13-710871-0 (PBK.)

Editorial/production supervision by Rita Young
Manufacturing buyer: Cathie Lenard

To my family—consultants all.

CONTENTS

ACKNOWLEDGMENTS

My sincere appreciation goes to the following people who contributed their time and knowledge to the making of this book:

Roland C. Cornelius
Consultant, Shipping

Harold G. Doherty
Consultant, Financial Services

Allan H. Eber
Consultant, International Trade

Jeanne Glennon
Publications Coordinator, Bank of America

Jack Handley
Senior Training Specialist, Corporate Training
Federal Reserve Bank of San Francisco

David G. Hurley
Vice President, Arthur D. Little, Inc.

Crystal A. Johnson
Consultant, Graphic Design

David Johnson
Assistant to the Chairman
Pacific Westbound Conference

Leo Maes
Assistant Vice President, Training Program Development
Bank of America

Richard T. Matthews, C.P.A.
Partner, Mann Judd Landau

Vincent McKenna
Sales, California State Automobile Association

William J. Murphy, Jr.
Consultant, Structural Engineering

Olga Paulsen
Consultant, Art Director

Robert C. Pehrson
Financial Consultant

Robert J. Person
Partner, National Director of Bank Consulting
Coopers & Lybrand

Henry W. Peterson
Consultant, Advertising

Carl Ricceri
Grant Specialist, U.S. Department of Commerce

A. Thomas Rohner
Manager, Public Relations
California State Automobile Association

Anne M. Schmid
Consultant, Medical Writer/Editor

Janis M. Zivic
Vice President, Heidrick and Struggles, Inc.

INTRODUCTION

WHAT IS A PRIVATE CONSULTANT?

A private consultant is a self-employed individual who, for a fee, gives experienced and skilled advice or service in a field of special knowledge or training. In the interest of accuracy, this definition might also include the following statement: A consultant is an advisor, a fixer, a boss, and a slave; a catalyst, a stabilizer, a listener, and a talker; a specialist and a generalist; a manager and a quasi-employee who works alone or with the client's staff. Consultants act as motivators and monitors; they also serve as work horses and stepping stones.

Consultants speak the technical language of both government and industry and work in every employment field. Consultants work in agriculture, astrology, banking, building, catering, criminology, engineering, exporting, and hundreds of other vocations and occupations. There is no job that cannot be done by a consultant.

Men and women of all ages and backgrounds are consultants. These people have two basic capabilities in common—a marketable skill and a determination to succeed.

HOW PRIVATE CONSULTING DIFFERS FROM FREE-LANCING

Although this text is addressed to private consultants, some of the advice may apply to free-lancers as well. Although both private consultants and free-lancers are self-employed and both sell their skills and experience, the consulting profession differs from free-lancing in the following ways:

- Consultants rarely sell a finished piece of work in advance of a contract. Free-lancers often work in anticipation of future sales. For example, writing and art consultants work under contract on assigned tasks, whereas free-lance writers and artists may create a piece of work and then try to sell the product.
- Consultants work for specific clients, in client-directed environments. Free-lancers usually control their own working conditions.
- Some consultants enter into partnerships and other business arrangements subject to licensing and government regulations. Free-lancers are usually the sole proprietors of their business.
- Consultants with more complex business arrangements may have higher overhead expenses for office and promotional costs than free-lancers.

THE GROWING NEED FOR PRIVATE CONSULTANTS

Over three fourths of the nation's private businesses call upon consultants to help them solve problems, open up new fields, get through peak work periods, recruit new employees, and carry out a variety of other tasks. Additionally, government agencies spend over $2 billion per year for consulting services. As the pressure to increase productivity continues to build, all sectors of business and industry are finding a greater need for the assistance and support of contract personnel with special skills.

Many consulting jobs are handled by teams of experts from large consulting firms who service all areas and levels of management. Although these firms strongly dominate the consulting market, the growing trend has been toward hiring individuals who maintain their own private consulting practice. Two factors account for this trend: (1) Some contracts awarded to consulting firms are being renegotiated and a portion of the work is being delegated to private consultants; and (2) As the value of using skilled private consultants becomes more widely understood, many small businesses are retaining individual practitioners. Thus, the demand for dedicated and skilled personnel in the private consulting profession is definitely on the increase.

HOW THIS BOOK CAN HELP YOU GET STARTED IN YOUR OWN CONSULTING PRACTICE

This book is published to help you understand how you can turn your experience into employment dollars by working in the growing profession of private consulting. If you have a marketable skill and are willing to invest the time and effort to learn a few essential marketing techniques and business practices, this book will provide the basic instruction needed to start you off on your own consulting career.

Chapter 1 discusses the temperament and background needed for success in the private consulting profession; important assets include education, experience, ethics, and financial backing.

Chapter 2 describes several types of services consultants offer, discusses a private consultant's clients and competitors, and outlines some of the advantages and disadvantages that go with private consulting work.

Other chapters offer step-by-step guidelines to advise you how to win clients, complete assignments, and run a profitable business.

Private consulting offers a continual challenge and presents opportunities for growth and advancement far beyond those of any job you might have working for others. Success in this profession is, however, in direct proportion to the amount of time and energy you put into performance. If you have the ambition and drive needed to succeed in this business, there is virtually no limit to how far you can go.

All the information on how to set up and maintain your own business is included on these pages. However, just reading this book will not make you a successful consultant. *You* must provide the initiative and energy needed to put the suggestions into motion.

1

STRENGTHS NEEDED
TO SUCCEED
IN PRIVATE CONSULTING

The private consulting profession needs people who are self-starters; who are articulate, alert, and aggressive; and who have a strong belief in their own abilities. To be a private consultant you should like variety, be willing to learn new skills, be able to adapt to change, and thrive on uncertainties. You also need tenacity, perseverance, and courage to keep going when proposals are rejected and assignments are hard to find. Consultants need physical stamina and energy to stand up under long hours of work when deadlines loom ahead and the stability and patience to remain calm when job pressures mount.

To be a private consultant you should like to work as an independent contractor, not an employee; you should enjoy seeking out your own assignments, writing your own contract agreements, billing for and collecting your own fees, and legally owning and managing your own business.

Private consulting is no ordinary job, but the profession does not attract ordinary individuals, either.

TALENTS NEEDED

In the course of your day-to-day activities as a consultant you will need a variety of talents to handle the many professional roles within a given job.

- *Competitor.* To find clients, win assignments, and build your practice, you will need to be a skilled competitor who enjoys business rivalry.

- *Strategist.* To initiate organizational planning, manage interactions between client partners who have opposite views, and maneuver work forces into positions of productivity, you will need the strategic ability of an army general.

- *Scholar.* To pursue facts, analyze needs, study the market, query new clients, track results, follow up on suggestions, and evaluate finished work, you will need an inquiring mind. A consultant should be a student who is always willing to learn.

- *Teacher.* To present program changes, launch new products, persuade publics, train new employees, and advise managers, you will need to be a skilled teacher.

- *Listener.* To hear what clients and resource people are really saying and discern their needs, you have to be the audience, the target for talk, the one who is told.

- *Communicator.* To write clear and understandable proposals, contracts, letters, and reports, and to be able to speak informatively, you should be a skilled reporter, writer, statistician, evaluator, and speaker.

- *Motivator.* Because you will seldom carry out an assignment entirely on your own, you will need to be skilled in persuasion so that you can enlist the help and cooperation of your clients and their resource people.

Consultants, indeed, must wear many hats, even the conical crown of a master magician. Although consultants should never promise miracles, they must seem to be performing them.

TEMPERAMENT NEEDED

To be successful in the consulting profession you will need the type of temperament that enables you to work with a variety of personalities under ideal as well as under impossible conditions, with rules that change daily while you wait for answers that never come. To manage the give-and-take of a consulting assignment you will need to be all of the following: *flexible* enough to change plans to please all types of clients and to work on every level of socio-economic need; *humble* enough to fit into a team of regular employees and, when needed, to pitch in and labor beside them on a task; *confident* enough of your own abilities to make decisions and lead others; *understanding* enough to recognize when other workers feel threatened; and *sincere* enough to win their cooperation.

CONSULTANT'S PERSONALITY TEST

Some people have a better chance to succeed in the consulting profession than others because they possess certain personality traits that help them promote their skills. Those individuals who have a high level of belief in their own abilities, work well with people, and are adaptable to change, make the best consultants.

If you are wondering how well you rate on these success factors, try the test that follows to discover your hidden character strengths and weaknesses. You may not know yourself as well as you think you do.

Low scores don't mean that you should give up on the idea of going into consulting. Scores are designed to help point out where you need to take steps to change your attitude. Use these scores as a guide to help you attain your career goals.

Reply to each question spontaneously without pondering the

different shades that could be developed on each side of a question. Keep track of your answers on a separate sheet of paper.

PART I. Self-Confidence

Answer either *Yes* or *No* to each question.

1. If called upon can you get the ball rolling at a business meeting?
2. Do you turn down new opportunities because you doubt your ability to handle them?
3. Can you state your opinions briefly?
4. Do you tend to put things off?
5. Would you rather work for one client all the time rather than change clients?
6. Do you prefer to talk to people in person when possible, rather than sending a memo?
7. Do you accept compliments gracefully?
8. Do you admit it and ask questions when you do not know something?
9. Do you speak up when you do not agree with an idea?
10. Do you face problems squarely and try to solve them?

Answers

1. Yes   You have confidence in yourself as a leader.
2. No   Confident people seek out new opportunities.
3. Yes   Rambling answers point to unsureness.
4. No   People who are sure of themselves find little reason to procrastinate.
5. No   Confident people enjoy meeting new clients.
6. Yes   A person who doesn't want to hold a discussion face-to-face sometimes hides behind a memo.
7. Yes   Confident people do not need excessive praise, but they are not embarrassed by genuine appreciation.
8. Yes   There is nothing wrong in admitting that you do not know something. This is the way to learn.
9. Yes   Confidence means believing in your own ideas.
10. Yes   A problem that is not faced can only lead to a feeling of frustration and inadequacy.

Scoring

10 correct answers: You're a natural!

8 or 9 correct answers: You occasionally lack confidence, but this is human. You'll make a good consultant.

7 or fewer correct answers: Perhaps you should have more positive experience working at a regular job before you go into consulting.

PART II. Ability to Get Along Well With Others

Answer whether you think statements are *True* or *False.*

1. People should be considered by their good points first.
2. Sharing your project plans with all involved employees can help progress.
3. For a consultant the art of listening is as important as talking.
4. It is always best to try to do your consulting work entirely by yourself.
5. Only principals in an agreement should be consulted about project problems.
6. In a position of authority you will lose respect if you admit that you are wrong.
7. You should not allow your emotions to influence you.
8. Consultants should act as onlookers and advisors rather than participants in actual assignment work.
9. Most people don't want to bother to try to solve problems.
10. People should be told when they are wrong.

Answers

1. True   People who see the good side in others are more apt to be good leaders.
2. True   Don't just talk with the boss. Let everybody in on what's going on.
3. True   Consultants who talk incessantly hear only their own opinions.
4. False   Seek out the help and cooperation of others who may add new dimensions to a project.
5. False   Anyone familiar with an assignment should be listened to. Sometimes it takes several voices to solve one problem.
6. False   Admitting you are wrong can be a way of saying you respect the knowledge and opinions of those you are working with.

7. False If you recognize the value of your own emotions, you will be more willing to accept the feelings of others.
8. False Consultants who get in and work as part of a team gain a better understanding of the project and get better cooperation from resource people assigned to assist.
9. False Most people are basically problem solvers and willingly help when asked.
10. False Just because a person takes a position opposite yours does not make this position wrong. The person may be supporting another perfectly acceptable answer.

Scoring

10 correct answers: You understand people and seem to have a genuine regard for their feelings. You'll make a great consultant.

8 or 9 correct answers: You'll still make a good consultant, but you could stand to loosen up a bit.

7 or fewer correct answers: Try getting out and talking with more people. Ask opinions and listen. This will make you a better leader.

PART III. Adaptability

Select one answer for each question.

1. What should you do when one of your ideas is rejected by a client?
    (A) Argue and try to win your point.
    (B) Accept the rejection and work out a new idea.
    (C) Quit the job.
2. What should you do about slipping deadlines?
    (A) Assign priorities.
    (B) Ignore your timetable.
    (C) Cut part of your program.
3. If a client company changes hands during the middle of a contract, what should you do?
    (A) Ask to be let out of the contract.
    (B) Meet with the new client and offer to adapt your contract to meet any new requirements.
    (C) Go right ahead with the work.
4. What should you do if you are asked to take over an assignment someone else has been unsuccessful with?
    (A) Accept the job and salvage what is usable.

(B) Refuse the job.

(C) Accept the job, discard everything that has been done and start fresh.

5. What should you do if you cannot agree with a client about fees?

    (A) Accept what you have been offered.

    (B) Refuse the job.

    (C) Try for benefits that will make up the difference.

6. What should you do if you find you are unable to carry out an assignment as specified in your contract?

    (A) Ask to be let out of the contract.

    (B) Tell your client about the problem and ask permission to work out an alternate plan.

    (C) Proceed until you can go no further then wait for orders.

7. What should you do if you bid on a job and are asked to work under another consultant?

    (A) Withdraw your bid.

    (B) Insist your bid stands as a single.

    (C) Accept the compromise assignment.

8. What should you do if you are asked to take a travel assignment?

    (A) Refuse to travel.

    (B) Go only if your fees are doubled.

    (C) Accept the assignment.

Answers

1. B   Consultants should accept client's rejection of ideas and substitute new ones.

2. A   Find out what the client wants done first and attack jobs in priority order.

3. B   Try to meet the needs of the new company and hope to win a new client who may offer future assignments.

4. A   If you salvage part of the work you can save your client time and money; this is always a plus when you seek another assignment from that client.

5. C   Maybe an office and a secretary or other similar resource help could be furnished by a client. This help could possibly net you more over the length of the contract than higher fees.

6. B   The consultant that saves the day by working out an alternate plan is more apt to get a second assignment.

7. C   If the pay is the same, simply consider the consultant your boss and ask to have this stated in your contract.

8. C   Travel assignments look good on your resume. They mean that you are worth sending a distance to solve a problem.

Scoring

7 or 8 correct answers: You make the most of changing situations and manage to be a good leader in spite of them.

6 or fewer correct answers: You're a bit inflexible. Try to practice making changes in plans until you get used to seeing both sides of any situation.

EDUCATION NEEDED

To qualify as an expert in almost any field of consulting some kind of education is needed. Your education may be formal, or you may be self-taught. No yardstick can measure the exact amount of schooling needed for any field of consulting. Every area of service differs from every other, and each requires a different type and level of education.

If, for example, you want to be a photography consultant, you will need considerable knowledge of film sensitivity, exposure control, and high-precision photographic instruments. You can become self-taught in this profession by studying the many excellent texts available and by then working with cameras, lenses, and film until you learn by trial and error. Your skill, however, must be equal to, or greater than, that of others in the profession, regardless of how you come by your knowledge.

In some professions you must be registered or licensed by the state or community in which you work. If, for example, you plan to be a consultant in structural engineering, you will need a civil engineering degree and a structural engineering license for the state in which you plan to practice. Testing determines those eligible for a license.

How to Determine
if You Have the Education Needed
to Be a Consultant
in Your Chosen Profession

The amount of education you will need in your chosen consulting profession depends upon how well you compare with other successful individuals already working in the field. Use these two qualifying measures to make the comparison.

1. Do you have the required education and licenses to practice your profession legally in your area? (To determine area prerequisites for your profession, consult local and state officials for licenses and educational certificates and degrees required.)

2. Is the level of your education equal to, or better than, that of others in your profession? (To ascertain the level of education of others in your profession, talk with practicing consultants and query members of established professional organizations in your field.)

If you are not familiar with the professional organizations in your area, the following books, found in the reference sections of many public libraries, may offer leads to names and addresses of organized groups.

Encyclopedia of Associations, Denise S. Akey, Editor. Published by Gale Research Company, Book Tower, Detroit Michigan 48226 (313/961-2242).

National Trade and Professional Associations and Labor Unions (U. S. and Canada), Craig Colgate, Jr., Editor. Published by Columbia Books Incorporated, 777 14th Street, N. W., Washington, D.C. 20005 (202/737-3777).

Weigh all answers to your inquiries, and then make a personal decision concerning whether your educational background is sufficient to qualify you as a consultant in the profession of your choice.

If you are educated in two fields, try to determine where your greater talent lies and practice only in that one area of business. You will weaken your service to clients and undermine your reputation if you spread yourself too thin by trying to function in too many areas.

When Should Education Cease?

Wise and judicious consultants make a point of never ceasing to try to learn. Seminars, corporate training sessions, night classes, and home study courses are the kinds of opportunities that bright, intelligent people with inquiring minds take advantage of regardless of how long they have been in business.

Consultants also learn from each assignment they accept. With every new client you can add to your technical knowledge and reinforce your ability to talk with, and help, others. You can learn from your successes and your mistakes. In consulting, nothing learned is ever wasted, and education should be an ongoing plan.

EXPERIENCE NEEDED

In recent years the trend has been toward earning advanced college degrees. Master's degrees and PhDs have become almost as common as high school diplomas were a century ago. While a high level of formal education might especially serve those individuals who plan to go into very specialized professions, advanced degrees are certainly not needed in all areas of business. Practical business sense, gained from working at day-to-day assignments, may have more to do with advancing in many consulting professions than advanced degrees.

The following examples illustrate how formal education was not enough to succeed as a consultant in one field and how practical experience led to success in another.

A journalism professor who held a number of degrees and taught at a large university decided to retire from the classroom and become a consultant. The professor's plan was to offer advice on format and content to small-town newspaper editors. The professor was strong on theory, but knew too little about the pressures of running a small publication to offer the kind of practical help editors would have found useful. The attempt to become a private consultant failed.

A high school dropout who went to work in a bookshop had better luck. This young person was inherently bright, ambitious, and hard-working. For ten years and in three different bookshops the young clerk worked and studied the book trade, learning what types of books sold the best, which displays attracted the most buyers, what kind of advertising brought in the most customers, and the way to manage a store the most profitably. One day the bookshop clerk decided to stop working for other people and start working as a consultant, teaching shop owners how to improve their businesses. Because the clerk knew client needs, this venture into the world of consulting was an outstanding success.

These two stories clearly illustrate that sometimes success is directly related to the practical experience you can apply to your client's needs, not to your education.

The Best Age
to Go into Consulting

There are no age limits in consulting work. You are ready and of sufficient age to go into consulting when:

- You are mature and confident enough to be able to advise others.
- You are educated and experienced enough to do the work.
- You have the health and stamina to do the work.
- You have the financial backing and contacts needed to get started.

Consulting can be a first job right out of school. Many graduates interested in consulting go to work for large management consulting firms when they need to gain experience before going into business for themselves. Consulting is a field that more and more young people are now entering.

Consulting can be a way for mid-career employees to get out of an unsatisfying job. Individuals who are tired of working in large corporations, where they seldom see the end result of their efforts, or in dead-end positions, where their talents are unused or misused, are now finding that consulting is a way to drop up instead of dropping out. Many mid-career employees who feel they have put in their time learning their skills are now quitting routine jobs and becoming their own full-time employer. These people have elected to use their remaining productive years to work for themselves rather than for a company.

Consulting can be a way for retirees to put their years of experience back to work. Most seniors are now finding that retirement, with its twenty-four hours per day of leisure time, is not as ideal as they once pictured. Many people who have retired from a company in a fanfare of farewell parties are now coming back just a short time later knocking on company doors, ready to start a second career as a consultant. And with spiraling inflation, many seniors are also finding that retirement funds may be inadequate and that they need the dollars they can earn as consultants to supplement their incomes. Many retirees work only part time and still enjoy increased leisure hours and less job pressure. From this older, competent, and qualified group of people come some of the profession's best workers.

Success in consulting in your chosen field is a combination of enough education to meet professional standards and requirements, enough experience to be able to help others, and the maturity to handle all client needs, questions, and problems wisely.

ETHICS

When you work for a company you must abide by company policies, work under conditions dictated by management, and be answerable to a supervisor. When you work as a private consultant you are accountable to yourself, you discipline yourself, and you devise your own professional working code of ethics. This is both a privilege and a responsibility.

Some consultants belong to professional associations and they work under the code of ethics and standards of conduct put forth by the members of that group. Incompetence or unethical practices may lead to expulsion from the association and can eventually lead to a loss of livelihood.

Most consultants, whether or not they belong to a professional association, feel that they have a moral obligation to support their profession by maintaining high ethical standards. Everyone associated with the profession benefits by this policy. The better the reputation of the profession as a whole, the greater the feeling of trust clients will have for each individual within that group.

In all their business dealings, professionals should strive to live by an ethical code founded on a keen sense of right and wrong. The code of ethics that follows is built upon that premise and is designed to serve consultants in every field.

A Consultant's Code

Consultants should work only where they are needed. When called in to make a proposal, you should give an honest opinion of the basic services needed, and if additional services might benefit the client, but are not essential, recommendations for these services should be added in a second section labeled *optional.*

For example, a training consultant, called in to introduce a new system to management, might recommend a second training session to be offered to regular employees as an optional service. The overall interests of the company would be served here by having all levels of personnel kept up to date on company systems.

Consultants should offer proposals only on those jobs they are qualified to undertake. If you lack the basic skills and experience to carry out an assignment on which you have been asked to make a proposal, decline the offer and explain your reasons.

Consultants should never contract for more work than they can manage well. When you take on several assignments at once and skip around from job to job, you are likely to confuse assignments or cut corners on your service. A better arrangement would be to take one assignment following another, booking them as they are requested. This plan gives you a chance to offer each client your undivided attention.

Consultants should establish a fee schedule that is fair and equal for all clients. Fee schedules should apply equally to all your clients regardless of company size or ability to pay. The only exceptions you should make to this rule are fees for nonprofit organizations and for government contract work where there are inherent limits.

Consultants should communicate directly with their clients should an error occur during the course of an assignment. Mistakes can't always be avoided, but they should never be covered up or blamed on someone else. As soon as you discover an error in your work you should tell your client and offer to make restitution. Whether your errors are the result of poor planning or the selection of faulty materials, you should make good any loss to the client on your own time. Not only is this a matter of ethics, but you are also legally liable if the client's business is damaged or someone is hurt as the result of an error or omission on your part.

Consultants should put their client's business interests ahead of their own. You owe it to your clients to speak well of them. You should decline an assignment rather than work on a project where you disapprove of the client or when you feel the work may undermine your own professional reputation. Freedom to choose assignments is one of the advantages of being a consultant. To work for a client says, in a sense, that you believe in what the client is doing. Don't work for someone you can't believe in.

Consultants should never disclose confidential information. With or without a confidentiality clause in your contract, you should never divulge information about a client or a client's work. Your conversation should be guarded even with the client's regular employees, who may not be privilege to information about your consulting assignment.

For example, a personnel consultant, hired by a company to recruit 100 new employees for the purpose of staffing a new office, should never disclose assignment details or numbers to anyone outside the company. A rival company could be tipped off to the projected expansion before information is released to the public.

Additionally, the personnel consultant should not discuss the project with employees within the company who have not been assigned to the work. Personnel within the organization, hearing that 100 people are being added to the staff, could start rumors that a whole department is being replaced or that present employees are being passed over for the new and better positions. Such news could lower employee morale and productivity.

Consultants should personally take charge of work signed for, unless otherwise stated in a contract. Work you have signed a contract to complete should never be given to another consultant without the knowledge and permission of the client. Additionally, all assistants hired by a consultant should be supervised by that consultant.

Consultants should not represent conflicting or competing interests without the consent of those concerned. You should make your client list an open book and never take on a new client if either that client or former clients will suffer by, or object to, the arrangement. This type of contention is known as a conflict of interest. When you represent two or more competitors, your clients may be concerned about the confidentiality of their business statistics. You may not be able to help being offered work by competing businesses, but you shouldn't take on contracts with them until you have a go-ahead from all parties.

An example of a situation involving conflicting interests might be the following: Bank A. hires an advertising writer to prepare some media advertising. Bank B. approaches the same consultant and offers a contract for work similar to what the consultant is doing for Bank A.

Before taking on the second contract the consultant should inform both clients of the dual role and get their approval to go ahead. Additionally, the consultant should assure both parties that there will be no similarity between the ideas presented and that all information will be kept separately and held in strictest confidence.

When conflicts do not influence your judgment or impair the quality of your service, they can be worked out harmoniously. In fact, clients can really benefit when you take several jobs with the same type of client. With each assignment you gain additional experience in the field and become more competent.

A second kind of conflict can arise when consultants recommend the purchase of merchandise they have for sale. A combination of a business ownership and a consulting service, in which the business relates to the type of consulting offered, is becoming quite common. Such business combinations, which prove very profitable, are usually the outgrowth of a business ownership. As consulting opportunities present themselves in the field relating to the business, many owners take on the second role of consultant as well.

Without real conflict you can recommend your own merchandise as part of your consulting advice if you honestly communicate the fact that you are acting in a dual role—as a consultant and as an owner-salesperson who will profit by a client purchase. For example, an interior decorator who works as a consultant and who also owns an antique shop might recommend the purchase of antiques from that shop. The client might well wonder if the consultant recommended the pieces only to make a sale.

You can handle this type of conflict and rarely run into a problem if you are completely candid about your interests as owner at the first business meeting with your client. The decorator-consultant, for example, would need to tell a client the following facts:

- The consultant also owns an antique shop.
- The consultant plans to recommend the purchase of pieces from that shop.
- Nothing will be recommended that is not in the very best interest of the client.
- The client is free to reject any purchase suggestions and still retain all other consulting services.

The client, now aware of the consultant's connection with the shop, may decide either to go ahead with a contract or to cancel it.

In any situation when you wish to sell to a client, direct communication concerning your personal gain by the sale should always be disclosed before any service is performed. If a client objects to purchasing from you as the consultant, the contract can be cancelled, or you can agree to recommend merchandise other than your own.

Honor is everything in the consulting business. A client must feel you can be trusted. Direct communication with a client about any conflict is the best way to honor a trust.

Less Formal Commitments

The following points should enable you to work well with others and feel good about yourself.

- Approach all assignments with enthusiasm.
- Take professional pride in your work.
- Never let success make you self-important.
- Help your colleagues by taking an interest in their problems and offering your support.
- Never encroach upon the employment of another consultant.
- Limit self-promotion to what is in keeping with the standards of others in your profession.

Consultants who gain a reputation for being trustworthy and conscientious are referred by one client to another, and their business thrives. But the second and somewhat hidden value in practicing good ethics is that when you live and work within such a code, you live in harmony with yourself as well.

FINANCIAL BACKING

An old proverb says, "If you wait to have children until you can afford them you will be childless." This theory might also apply to starting your own consulting business. Those individuals who think they have to pile up a small fortune before they can start out on their own will probably never cut their ties with a regular employer. Fear of failure, of going under, deters a lot of prospective consultants from ever finding out about being in business for themselves. Quitting a job with steady pay to gamble on an unsure future can be a big step, particularly for people who are responsible for the support of others in a family. But if you definitely want to be a consultant, if you want that chance to be your own boss, by all means try. Even if your venture is a failure and you have to drop back to working for someone else, you'll be better for trying.

Earning and saving the money needed to start your own business will call for some planning and maybe even some sacrifice. But if you attain your goal of financial independence, the outcome will be worth the struggle. Begin your plan for independence by making a personal financial assessment. Draw up a list of your assets and liabilities to find out where you stand financially. The answer will tell you how far you have to go to clear up old debts before you can begin to save the money to start your consulting business. Here are some typical assets you may have:

- cash on hand
- bank accounts, certificates, or investments
- pay for work in progress
- equity in a home or other real property
- an automobile, boat, or trailer
- furniture and other household equipment
- jewelry

You may owe more money than you think if you haven't put your liabilities down on paper. Some liabilities you may have are:

- current bills
- notes, mortgages, or car payments
- taxes and insurance payments
- rent and other household expenses
- dues and licenses

Add up your assets and then your liabilities, and weigh one against the other. If you are deeply in debt and you have no assets it would be practical to liquidate (for instance, you don't want to sell the bed you sleep on), you had better work out a budget and a savings plan to get yourself out of debt before you leave a salaried position. There *are* some assets that it would be practical to liquidate to help pay off your debts. For example, if you have two automobiles, consider selling one if you can get along without it. Selling a car can help cut expenses in two ways. You'll save the cost of insurance and upkeep on a second car, and you'll also save finance charges on those bills you pay off.

Once you know where you stand financially you can go ahead with a plan to back yourself in business. Self-backing may mean you will have to delay your move into self-employment while you save the sum needed to get started, but starting loan-free can be worth the wait.

Backing Yourself

Open a savings account and then follow this step-by-step plan to financial independence.

1. Determine your monthly cost of living. Be sure to add in taxes, insurance payments, and an emergency fund.
2. Determine your monthly income. Be sure to add in items such as interest earned and income contributed by other members of your family.
3. Subtract your monthly living expenses from your monthly income. The difference is the amount you can add to your savings each month.
4. Estimate how much cash you will need to supply an office and buy professional equipment. Even a home office has to have files, record books, stationery, and supplies; nearly all consultants need some kind of equipment to do their work.
5. Estimate what your monthly business overhead will be. This should include items such as insurance, transportation, accounting services, and promotional costs.
6. Add together your estimated startup costs, plus two months business overhead and two months basic living expenses. The total will give you the amount you will need to save before you can terminate your salaried position and go into private consulting.
7. Divide the total amount you need in savings by the amount you are able to save each month to determine the number of months needed to reach your goal of independence. For example, if you can save $200 each month and you determine your savings need to be $3,000, you will have to save for fifteen months to reach your goal. The computation will be as follows:

$3,000 to be saved ÷ $200 put aside monthly = 15 months to goal

Enlist the support of your family in meeting the financial goal. Everyone in your household can help by cutting expenses. Your family can be of help in another way, too. Some of them can help earn additional income. Even young people who want spending money or need new clothes can go to work and earn extra cash.

Loans

If you have a large family or other financial obligations that require every cent of your income, you may not be able to save enough to back yourself in business. In this case you may want to consider the possibility of taking out a loan. Here are three loan sources to explore.

Friends or family.   A friend or a family member may have enough confidence in you to become a nonworking partner in your business. This type of partner puts up the cash while you do the work. You may be able to discharge your loan after a period and become the sole proprietor.

Private lending institutions.   Banks, credit unions, and other private lending sources still make a limited number of loans to people starting out in business. However, money for this type of loan is tight. In addition, most bank loans must be secured by mortgages on property or by pledges of stocks, bonds, or other collateral. Unsecured loans are available only to individuals whose credit standing is well established by a history of successful borrowing.

A bank loan must be retired according to a predetermined schedule, so whether your business earns any money or not your loan payment has to be met. If you put up your house as collateral, you could lose the roof over your head if your business is slow in getting started.

Government institutions.   If you have been turned down for a loan by a bank or any other private lending institution, you may qualify for financing from a public sector. The U.S. Small Business Administration has a loan program for which you may be eligible. Here again money is tight. Few funds are now available, and loans take several months for approval, but applying for public funding is always worth a try.

Other Financial Arrangements

If saving money or obtaining a loan just isn't possible for you, maybe one of the following suggestions will be workable for a limited time:

If you are married, get your spouse to support you while your business is getting started. Many couples have this arrangement for getting through school, and it can work just as well for getting started in a business.

Take a part-time job and work at consulting in the other half of your time. Maybe your part-time job could be in the evening so you would be free to work days as a consultant. Whatever type of part-time work you do should allow flexible hours. For example, you might register with a temporary employment service and go out on jobs when you aren't doing consulting work.

Keep a full-time regular job and moonlight at consulting on weekends and evenings until you attain a regular client list. To make this kind of arrangement work, your clients must be willing to hire your services at odd hours. Again, if you have a regular job in the evenings you can work days as a consultant, but physically this kind of schedule can be terribly wearing if you keep it up for too long.

2

THE NATURE
OF THE WORK

The actual work that consultants perform is sometimes misunderstood by the very individuals who could profit from the service of a consultant. Some employers look on consultants as "free loaders" who charge a fee for telling managers something they already know. Others look on consultants as "wave makers" whose function is to spy on regular employees and recommend mass layoffs. Still others think of consultants as "miracle workers" who can achieve the impossible when everyone else has failed.

None of these descriptions is accurate. Consultants work hard to understand and solve client problems. They try to respond to questions with helpful answers, boost productivity, and turn out a product. Consultants continue to be hired, and their ranks are growing, because employers who understand their services know that these professionals can aid their business and save them money.

SPECIFIC SERVICES CONSULTANTS OFFER

Operations. An operations assignment involves supervision and assistance with work in progress. This is the type of service most frequently requested by clients. Consultants may work along with a client's regular staff, with hired assistants, or alone. The end product of an operations assignment is finished work. For example, some end products of an operations assignment might be manufactured goods, a completed design, accounting work, or a finished construction.

Investigation. An investigation assignment involves review of work in progress to determine needs. Consultants must investigate records, conduct interviews, and make site visits. The end product of an investigation assignment is a report of findings and specific recommendations for any action needed. The report may be used to settle a dispute, justify rate hikes, decrease or increase personnel, untangle delaying confusion, settle legal battles, or solve insurance questions. Consultants may also appear before review boards or in court on behalf of clients.

Feasibility studies. An assignment to do a feasibility study involves research and in-depth interviews. The end result of this type of assignment may be a decision on the value of a product or project. Examples of feasibility studies are determinations such as whether a proposed product will market well, whether a change in work flow will increase employee productivity, or whether a factory expansion will measurably increase profits. The end product of a feasibility study is a written report of findings and recommendations for possible action.

Procurement. A procurement assignment involves doing a study to evaluate a proposed purchase. Purchases under consideration might include land, buildings, equipment, materials, or securities. The end product of a procurement assignment is a written report and purchase recommendation. If the report is favorable to purchase, the client may hire the continued services of the consultant to arrange the acquisition.

Recruitment. A recruitment assignment involves the recruiting, interviewing, testing, and hiring of personnel. The end product of a recruitment assignment is prospective or actual hiring of new employees.

Training.   A training assignment may involve designing client training programs and doing the actual teaching. Instruction may include orientation of new personnel and introduction of new procedures, products, or equipment. The end products of a training assignment are training programs and trained personnel.

Planning.   A planning assignment involves designing a plan, including timetables and budgets, for endeavors such as program expansions, mergers, new procedures, or policy revisions. The end product of a planning assignment is a plan.

Testing.   A testing assignment involves conducting an area test to determine things such as personnel efficiency, equipment safety, or product quality. The end product of a testing assignment is a written report of test results.

Survey.   A survey assignment can involve the appraisal of a physical site by using instruments or the taking of an opinion poll by using samples and questionnaires. These studies may help clients in activities such as determining insurance needs, setting new rates, or settling court proceedings. The end product of a survey assignment is a written report on the completed survey.

The examples cited describe only some of the services consultants perform. Other skills in management, finance, engineering, health care, construction, agribusiness, environmental protection, and systems design, just to name a few, can also be provided by consultants.

Job Examples

For every business problem or need, an opportunity arises for a consultant. A few typical examples of situations for which consultants might be needed include the following:

During peak-load periods.   Tax consultants, for example, might be called in to assist a controller's regular staff just before tax reports are due.

When staff is temporarily insufficient.   Staff retirements, illness absenteeism, and summer vacation vacancies bring assignments to some consultants.

When a new area office is being opened.   Consultants who specialize in recruitment and training of employees can help clients who must hire new staff.

When management log jams need breaking up or labor disputes must be settled.   Personnel specialists, labor relations experts, and management evaluation consultants who are experienced in arbitration can bring opposing sides together.

To introduce a new product or service.   Consultants who specialize in promotional advertising, public relations, marketing profiles, product control, and product testing can provide technology and guidance when new products are being introduced.

To study investment possibilities.   Financial experts who specialize in expenditures can help with investment evaluations and make purchase recommendations.

To cut down on shoplifting.   Security consultants can analyze store layouts and assign supervision where it is needed.

Specialists and Generalists

A specialist consultant practices in a limited field using highly specialized skills. For example, a writing consultant who writes only speeches would be considered a specialist in that field. Specialists can usually charge more for their services, but they are limited to the number of clients who need those services. A generalist writing consultant offers broader and more varied services. For example, a generalist consultant might write training manuals, news releases, articles, advertising copy, *and* speeches.

HOW TO DETERMINE YOUR SPECIFIC CONSULTING AREA

A person educated and experienced in a multi-faceted profession might wish to specialize in one particular area of that profession. For example, a systems engineer might wish to work at strategic planning. That same person might be able to do consulting work in product development, marketing, or field service. To determine your specific consulting area you should ask yourself the following questions:

In what area do I have the greatest interest?
In what area do I have the strongest aptitude?
Where is the greatest need for service?

If your preferred field of service is the one in which you have the strongest aptitude and where client need is strong, you'll have no problem deciding what kind of consulting work you should do. But, should you have a strong aptitude and interest in an area with few clients and a plethora of competition, you will need to give strong, practical consideration to a second choice. Picking a field to work in is really a process of eliminating the negatives.

CLIENTS—WHO THEY ARE AND WHY THEY HIRE

Clients have problems that need to be solved. Clients are people who need the knowledge and specific technologies of a professional. They are usually experts at their own business, but sometimes they need additional resources and specialized capabilities to help with that business. Clients can be found in all areas of government, business, industry, science, and the arts and can include the U.S. government, foreign governments and businesses, giant corporations, small businesses, colleges and institutions, or individuals working on their own. Anyone with a job that needs doing is a potential client. Anyone who hires a consultant is a client. Even consultants can be clients.

CLIENT'S RESPONSIBILITIES

Consultants are expected to give the best of their talents to their clients, to work diligently for each one, and to charge fair and professional fees for their services.

In turn, consultants have a right to expect their clients to deal fairly with them in matters of selection, professional cooperation, and prompt payment. A client's responsibilities can be spelled out very specifically in a formal contract, but more often than not, consultants merely hope that their clients will deal with them in good faith.

The basic responsibilities a consultant should be able to expect a client to fulfill are enumerated here in detail. This list may help you to choose your future clients, for certainly the better your client list, the more apt you will be to carry out your assignments successfully.

A client should abide by standard professional business practices in the following areas of responsibility:

- *Selection.* A client should select a consultant on the basis of the consultant's experience, ability, and the bid submitted. Clients should never allow personal or political influences to come between them and the fair selection of a consultant. Merit should be the final deciding factor in the selection of a consultant.

- *Professional courtesy.* A client should work with a consultant in a manner that is both courteous and respectful, listening to the consultant's advice and suggestions and acting upon them promptly.

- *Approvals.* A client should adopt a timely and uncomplicated approval system for answering questions, endorsing plans, and meeting deadlines. No matter how many people are involved in an approval committee, one person should always be available and responsible for consultant contact.

- *Information.* A client should trust a consultant with confidential information and furnish all necessary facts and figures needed to complete a project. Where research is required, special resource people should be assigned on a top priority basis to help with the delivery of this information.

- *Supplies and equipment.* Where so agreed, a client should furnish supplies and equipment needed to complete a consulting assignment. Supplies should be as requested by the consultant with substitutions made only upon approval. Equipment furnished should be in good repair and adequate to do the work.

- *Errors and omissions.* A client should communicate any dissatisfaction with a project directly to a consultant before discussing the matter with other employees. A consultant should be given a chance to explain delays, correct errors, or complete work that may have been left undone before a payment penalty is assessed.

- *Recommendations.* A client should credit a consultant for work done well, and in all situations speak well of a consultant before other employees. When opportunities present themselves a client should be willing to recommend a consultant to other business associates.

- *Payment.* A client should pay fees promptly in accordance with the contract schedule. Agreed-upon expenses, enumerated and backed by receipts, should be reimbursed promptly without question.

COMPETITORS

Competitors won't hurt your business; in fact, competition often helps bring more assignments your way. Any time a competent consultant completes an assignment satisfactorily the reputation of the profession as a whole is enhanced. Clients who have positive consulting experiences are likely to call on consultants again.

Competition is healthy. With many competitors in a profession, standards tend to rise and fees are lowered. This can actually be a help to your business. High standards build the reputation of the consulting profession as a whole. Reasonable fees make consulting work available to more businesses, and this in turn may increase your opportunity to find work.

A private consultant's competitors range from other private consultants all the way to giant, world-wide consulting firms. At some time in your private consulting career you may compete with, or work with, all of them. Generally, an individual practitioner's competition are the following:

Other individual practitioners.   The private consulting profession is growing; every year more people are realizing the advantages of going into business for themselves. Some areas of the profession are becoming crowded, but skilled consultants who market their services well can still find assignments. Other private consultants are the most formidable competition, but these colleagues can also help you in your business as well.

Small consulting firms.   A trend in progress is for two or three private consultants to band together and form partnerships or small consulting firms. In many cases this type of arrangement has proven quite successful. Partners can pool client lists, share office space, and even buy more and better equipment. This arrangement also allows individual partners to specialize in one aspect of the work. Small firms offer vigorous competition to individual practitioners.

General consulting firms.   A firm with a staff of consultants who are experts in several different professional capabilities is considered a general consulting firm. Clients with assignments that require a number of working disciplines may call upon a general consulting firm. Individual practitioners would be unable to handle such assignments singly, so they usually do not compete with general firms.

Full-service consulting firms.   Full-service firms offer an even broader range of professional capabilities than general firms. Most full-service firms have a large number of professional sections, and some have offices throughout the world. Occasionally these firms hire a private consultant who is skilled in a highly esoteric area to supplement their staff on certain assignments. However, private consultants rarely compete with full-service consulting firms.

Specialist consulting firms.   Firms that handle only one type of assignment—executive search, for example—are known as specialist firms. These firms may refer clients who need help not included in their speciality to other consulting firms or to individual practitioners. Specialist consulting firms range in size from two partners to world-wide organizations.

   The following reference book, found in the reference sections of many public libraries, lists consulting firms by state or foreign country and gives the company name and nature of business: *Consultants and Consulting Organization Directory,* Paul Wasserman, Managing Editor, published by Gale Research Company, Book Tower, Detroit, Michigan 48226.

Competitors Can Help You

On a day when you lose an assignment to a competitor you might wish you had no competition, but without colleagues you would also miss out on a number of benefits. Competitors keep you at your best. When you compete for clients you must keep your knowledge updated and your skills sharp.

Your competitors also provide a pattern of success for you to follow. You can learn how to present a proposal, set fees, or handle other steps of an assignment by watching the experts in your profession.

Your competitors may refer a client to you for assignments they are too busy to take. Like many other businesses, consulting has its workflow peaks and valleys. What may be a slow season for you could be an overload period for your competition. Other consultants may refer clients to you for work they cannot handle or for jobs outside the area of their specialty. Your competitors also may stand in for you when you have too many assignments. During those times when you have too much work you may want to recommend one of your colleagues to help your clients.

Your competitors may be willing to loan you special equipment or books relating to your mutual area of practice. Some consultants who may not wish to go into active partnerships do combine resources and purchase equipment to use on a sharing basis. And some consultants, even though they may be in different professions, share office space and secretarial help.

Your Attitude
Toward Your Competition

To deride a colleague's efforts or make negative statements about a competitor's work is never wise. Even if a client runs down your competition, never join in. Sniping adds nothing to your stature. Try to build on what has been done by others rather than deprecate their efforts. Instead of deriding a competitor, try to change a negative conversation around with lead sentences such as: "Let's see what I can do," or "This is an excellent point, now let's see if we can build on what has been done."

To paraphrase the Golden Rule: "Treat your competitors the way you hope they will treat you." A positive attitude on your part can lead to a positive working relationship with your client.

How to Meet Other Consultants in Your Profession

Getting to know other consultants in your profession offers some viable business advantages and may include a bonus of real friendships as well. If you live in an urban area and are willing to make an effort, meeting other consultants is relatively easy. Here are three ways to make contact with your professional colleagues.

1. Contact them on the job. Make an effort to get to know other consultants working for your client on the same assignment or other assignments.

2. Join professional organizations. Many professions have their own specialized groups who meet to talk shop, exchange general information, and report on market conditions. Many of these groups also establish educational requirements and maintain standards of conduct for their profession. (See Chapter 1 for the titles of two reference books offering names and addresses of organized groups.)

   Visit organizations active in your area and join one or two that meet at a time convenient for you to attend. If no group has been established for your profession in your area, start one.

3. Attend classes and special training sessions for people in your profession. The classroom is one of the best places to meet other consultants. People who are active and interested enough in their profession to want to further their education should make excellent candidates for colleague acquaintanceships.

ADVANTAGES CONSULTANTS ENJOY

Private consultants can pursue a job while enjoying the excitement of the chase; they can write a proposal and find satisfaction in creating a project plan. They can work where needed—where their opinions are sought and their ideas are acted upon. Consultants are free to enjoy a variety of specialized learning experiences within a kaleidoscope of changing work environments. They can select the clients they want to work for and decide the hours they want to work. Consultants need not wait for salary increases; they can set their own fees. Private consultants are their own bosses.

Specifically, consulting work offers these important advantages.

- Pay relative to what you know and the effort you put forth.
- A chance to use all your special talents while working at a variety of assignments where your skills are kept updated.
- The opportunity to be a leader instead of a follower, to be listened to, and to have your suggestions acted upon.
- The privilege of living in an area where you want to live, not where you have to live because you work there.
- The opportunity to meet the motivators and innovators in your field.
- The chance to gain new experiences and add to your skills, vocabulary, and knowledge with each new assignment.
- Freedom from unwanted job transfers and cross-country moves.
- The chance to work only where you are needed and where you are appreciated.
- The freedom to choose the time of day and the number of hours you wish to work each day as long as you accommodate your client.
- The choice of working at the hours you are at your mental and physical peak.
- The opportunity to set your own employment goals and advance at your own speed, since your success is in direct proportion to the personal effort you expend.
- Acceptance on the basis of what you know, since private consulting offers increasing opportunities for men and women who can demonstrate proficiency.

Consulting work offers some secondary advantages too, and sometimes these minor benefits can be the sweetest. Consultants who work at home some days or who have complete control over their working hours can

- Decide that the "dress code" for a day of work at home is an old sweater.
- Stay at home on a day when the sun is irresistible or when bad weather looms threateningly.
- Take a two-hour lunch break and sit on a bench in the park.
- Take a vacation without ever having to worry about a signup sheet.
- Ignore office politics.

The following statement typifies the way many consultants feel about the advantages of their jobs:

> Private consulting hardly seems like work. I do what I like to do; people listen to what I have to say; and I take time off when I want to. Best yet, I'm making more money than I ever did when I was working for someone else.

CONSULTING PITFALLS

Private consulting work is rewarding and interesting, and no one should be disheartened about the possibilities the profession has to offer, but it would be unfair to paint a picture of this type of employment as being all "sweetness and light." The problems and drawbacks that go with private consulting work are all too real, and too common, to ignore. The unwary can stumble into pitfalls along the path to professional success. At the very least these snares could decrease your productivity. At the very worst they could measurably damage your reputation and ruin your business.

Pitfalls are offered here not to discourage you but rather to offer suggestions on ways to lighten their impact or to avoid them altogether. Any problem has the potential of being serious if ignored. While some situations elude complete solution, an attempt at solving a difficulty may go a long way toward rendering it less harmful. For this purpose, the three different categories of work problems inherent in most private consulting work are defined and discussed here. These three categories are client-generated problems, general work problems, and personal work problems.

Client-Generated Problems

Getting along with your clients is basic to remaining employed as a consultant, but even with the most amiable of clients problems can sometimes crop up. At the first indication that a problem is brewing you should make every effort to find a quick solution. The earlier a solution is sought the sooner vital work flow can continue or good relations can resume. Sometimes answers can be quite simple, as the following examples illustrate:

CLIENT-GENERATED PROBLEM	CONSULTANT'S SOLUTION
Offer of pay lower than your quoted fee schedule.	Explain that you have a standard fee schedule that you consider fair for all clients. If the client is not willing to pay your asking price, decline the job.
Finding fault with minor details and slowing work progress by continually asking to have portions of work done over.	Try to satisfy clients with one correction per problem, and then remind them that deadlines are slipping.
Slow approvals.	Break up logjams with repeat memos and personal visits to those personnel who are late with answers.
Failure to furnish data and information needed.	Get a contract agreement on resource help.
Resentful staff employees.	Ask client to allay staff members' fears by explaining your position.
Ignoring consultant's project recommendations.	Remind client that you cannot be responsible for the outcome of a project when directives are ignored.
Late pay.	Bill tardy clients often and assess carrying charges after a set period of time.
Theft of ideas.	Protect your unused ideas with contract clauses.
Imposition on your personal time.	Define your work hours in your contract and be available for extra time on an emergency basis only.
Unethical practices.	Decline to take an assignment.

General Work Problems

Some problems such as pressure, the need for record keeping, and uneven work flow are inherent in the private consulting profession. But many of these problems and uncertainties also have remedies.

GENERAL WORK PROBLEMS	CONSULTANT'S SOLUTION
The need to keep up with correspondence.	Draft standard letters that meet your most frequent needs. Make minor, personalized changes for each client.

GENERAL WORK PROBLEMS	CONSULTANT'S SOLUTION
Uneven work flow.	Keep busy during slack times with continuing education. When jobs pile up, try to get a client to wait for you or recommend a colleague to take your place.
Having to record expenses.	Set up a recording system and keep to it until noting expenses becomes an in-bred habit.
The continual task of having to find new clients.	Set up an ongoing marketing plan that keeps you seeking new clients even when your assignment calendar is full.
Long assignments that create loss of objectivity on one job, outdated knowledge of other areas of work, and a reduced client list.	Market your services to a variety of clients who offer jobs of short to medium length.
Unknowns that crop up, change the complexity of an assignment and cause delays.	Be flexible enough to revise plans to save time. If delays cannot be made up, fall back on the contingency clause in your contract.

Personal Work Problems

Private consulting calls for a lot more involvement of your personal time than regular employment and requires you to be responsible for traditional employer tasks and moral obligations.

PERSONAL WORK PROBLEMS	CONSULTANT'S SOLUTION
Lack of company fringe benefits.	Set up your own benefit plans for health care, insurance, and retire-ment.
No regular paycheck.	Since consultants usually receive higher pay than regular employees, you should save during flush times for lean periods.
The loneliness of never belonging to a regular office team.	Join a professional group that meets in your area.

PERSONAL WORK PROBLEMS	CONSULTANT'S SOLUTION
Travel and long hours.	Define work hours in your contract and accept only those travel assignments that are not too lengthy.
Getting started with little or no money coming in.	Delay going into consulting until you have saved enough to cover living expenses and overhead for your first two months.
Taxes not withheld.	Set up a savings account to cover amount needed for taxes and deposit on a regular basis. Because taxes are not withheld by employers, consultants can keep tax money in a savings account until needed for payment, and earn interest on these funds.
Need to continue education.	Have a long-range plan that allows you to take advantage of seminars, classes, and other information-gathering opportunities.
Conflict of interest.	Decline any job in which conflicts cannot be resolved.

3

**WINNING
ASSIGNMENTS**

A PLAN FOR MARKETING YOUR SERVICES

When you are beginning as a consultant, a marketing plan to win assignments is mandatory—unless you are so well known that clients will begin knocking at your door the day you announce you are in business. Such a plan involves a threefold effort:

- Defining your skills and services and packaging this definition for presentation.
- Targeting your prospective clients.
- Personally contacting those clients.

Such an ambitious marketing plan which calls for a commitment of time and labor on your part, can bring excellent results.

Define Your Skills and Services

Start your marketing plan by making a list of your talents, educational achievements, and experience in your chosen profession. Talents, for example, might include an ability in medical records transcription, media research, or sheet metal fabrication and design. Under education, in addition to your basic schooling, which includes certificates and degrees, you should list the special awards, honors, and hours of technical training you have to your credit. Experience should include a list of your former employers and your positions with those employers. This comprehensive list will be used to write your special consultant's resume. This document will form the basis of your marketing presentation to prospective clients.

In writing your list, take care to leave out nothing of importance. The more precisely you define your skill, the more specialized service you can offer. Specialists are usually first in demand when a client has problems. Red Adair, for example, isn't just a firefighter—he's a specialist who quells oil-drilling fires. His services are sought out halfway around the world.

Write a Consultant's Resume

Use your list of skills and services to write a consultant's resume. Format for this type of resume differs from those used by people seeking full-time employment. Consultants may put greater emphasis on their special skills and describe client assignments rather than list former employers. However, if you are a new consultant with no client experience, list your prior employment until your client list grows; then rewrite your resume regularly to add the names of new clients and eliminate nonconsulting employment. Keep your resume short and easy to read by deleting less important contracts as you have more significant assignments to add.

Start your resume with a list of your areas of special service, which tells prospective clients what you can do to help them. Follow this section with your client list, and then name two or three former employers. Last of all, briefly state your education credits. Type your resume or have it typeset on your consultant's stationery and have a limited number of copies printed.

The following example (Figure 1) illustrates the type of information that should be included in your resume. Italic type is used to emphasize assignment content. Note the brevity of the prior employment list.

FIGURE 1. Consultant's resume.

```
                        BRADLEY L. MURPHY
                        Editorial Consultant
            555 Market Street, San Francisco, CA 94110

                        (415/555-6060)


AREAS OF SPECIAL SERVICE:

            Writing - Rewriting - Editing

                  Films              Reports
                  Training Programs  Brochures
                  Speeches           Articles

EMPLOYMENT:
                  January 1975 to Present:
                  Self-employed as an Editorial Consultant

            Principal Clients:

                  Lamont Savings Bank - San Francisco, CA
                  Training films and manuals

                  Allen & Ross, Advertising - Oakland, CA
                  Prospective client brochures
                  Speeches
                  Orientation film

                  James Associates, Investment - Los Angeles, CA
                  Training programs
                  News articles
                  Quarterly reports

                  Land & Fuller, International Accountants
                  Advertising film
                  Annual report
                  Speeches

                  Wilmington Savings and Loan - San Francisco, CA
                  Annual and quarterly reports
                  Training manuals

                  Williams Bros., Publishers - Hollywood, CA
                  Advertising copy
                  Technical editing

            Prior to 1975:

            Lamont Savings Bank - Senior Economic Editor
            Freemont Advertising Agency - Senior Copywriter

EDUCATION:
            University of California - BA Degree
            UCLA - Graduate Work, Films
```

Target Your Prospective Clients

Once you have listed your special skills and services and have written your consultant's resume, take your marketing plan one step further by making a list of those individuals and companies who might be your prospective clients. In addition, ask your former employers, professional associates, and others in the business community who know you, to help suggest names of clients who might be interested in your services. People who have heard of your work or who have worked with you in the past are your best source of information because they know your talents well. Don't hesitate to call these people and inform them of your decision to go into private consulting. Tell these contacts about the services you plan to offer, and let them know when you will be available. Telling people about your new career and asking for their help is one of the best ways to get your client list started. Even if some people are unable to offer immediate suggestions for your client list, they may call you with leads at a later date, or they may be interested in hiring you themselves.

Other good sources of eligible names for your prospective client list are the trade papers and periodicals directed to your profession. Reading these publications will keep you up to date on business trends and developments. This information could lead to clients. For example, an advertising consultant might learn about companies who will be awarding new media contracts or a construction engineer might see an announcement of plans for area development in special journals relating to their professions. Either announcement might lead to an assignment.

Make Contact with Your Prospective Clients

Once you have refined your list of prospective clients, your next step is to make personal contact with these people to offer your services. Making contact is often a four-step process, which includes:

- Introducing yourself and your service by letter.
- Following up your letter with a phone call asking for an appointment to meet with your prospective client.
- Making a personal call to introduce yourself and further explain your services.

- Following up your interview with a thank-you letter and a final offer of service.

Introduce yourself by letter. A letter is the best way to make a first contact with a prospective client. Even people who have known you need to be informed that you are now a private consultant and are interested in working for them. Besides serving as a written introduction, letters often get you past otherwise closed doors. Consultants who take the time to write and ask for an appointment are more frequently granted an interview than those who merely phone in their request or drop by unexpectedly.

Although it is understood that each individual letter to a prospective client should be freshly typed on your consultant's stationery, you can develop a model letter that can be slightly changed to personalize your message so your words fit nearly every prospective client situation. Your basic letter should contain the following:

- An introduction of yourself as a private consultant, a brief mention of your background, and a list of your professional services
- An expression of interest in working for the person or the company
- A request for a personal appointment to further describe your services
- A notice that you will follow up your letter with a phone call to inquire about a convenient time and date for the appointment. (The promised call relieves the person from the duty of answering your letter.)
- A final note that you are looking forward to a meeting in the near future.

State the reason for writing your letter within the first two sentences. For example, don't make small talk when you send a query letter to a prospective client. State that you are seeking new clients and would like an appointment to talk about working for the company. Couch your letter in a positive tone, as if rejection is not a possibility. To supply your reader with background information always include your consultant's resume and mention its inclusion so the second sheet won't be overlooked. Only a few letters should be sent out each week, so that follow-up is possible. Figure 2 is an example of an introduction letter to a prospective client.

How your letter looks when it goes out in the mail is of vital importance. A prospective client may judge you on this single piece of paper since your letters meet your clients before you do and they

```
              GEORGE SMITH - CONSULTANT

                  OFFICE INTERIORS
                    4555 Coleman
                San Francisco, CA 94112
                    415/555-3465


                                      September 2, 198x

    Andrew Landow, President
    LANDOW MANUFACTURING
    7432 Mosley
    San Francisco, CA 94124



    Dear Mr. Landow:

               During the coming busy days when your company is
    planning on opening two new offices in the San Francisco area,
    I would like to offer my professional services to advise and assist
    you with this undertaking.

               I am a private consultant specializing in the design
    and finishing of office interiors.   I have a degree in interior
    design and ten years background experience working in the profession.
    To give you additional information about my background I have enclosed
    a brief resume.

               If you could give me a brief period of time to talk
    with you I could explain further how I can be of service to your
    company.  I will be calling you within a few days to ask for an
    appointment.

               I look forward to meeting with you in the near future.


                                   Sincerely,

                                   George Smith
                                   George Smith


    Encl:
```

FIGURE 2. A sample introduction letter.

convey your important first impression for you. If your letters are
sloppy or inaccurate, a client may decide that your work will reflect
this same lack of attention. Your letters are your representatives in
the mail; let them speak well of you.

- Your letter should be well set up and typed without errors. If you cannot do this work yourself, hire someone to do the work for you. Letters are an important part of doing business.
- Date your letters and include the dates of any time periods referred to.
- Check your letters for errors in typing, grammar, punctuation, and spelling.
- Keep your copy brief and clear and avoid obsolete wording.
- Use courtesy in every line, tailoring your requests to the convenience of your client.

Let your letter, by its appearance, say you are a person who attends to business properly.

Follow up your letter with a phone call. Keep your appointment calendar clear for meeting dates, and after a period of four days— enough time for local letters to have arrived—follow up your letter with the promised phone call. You may have to call several times before you get through to the person you wish to speak to, but be persistent. You can't get an assignment if you don't make a contact.

When the prospective client comes on the line, introduce yourself by name and profession. Mention the fact that you have sent a letter and a resume. Ask if you may come in at a convenient time to talk about possible assignments.

If prospective clients say they don't need a consultant, ask if they know of anyone who might need your talents. They may name their competitors, who may or may not already be on your mailing list. They may give you a new lead. Ask if you may use their names as reference and follow up on the lead by letter and phone call.

If you are turned down in an attempt to make a contact, put that person's name at the bottom of your list. You may want to try the same person or a different person in the company at a later date.

Make personal visits. If you are successful in making an appointment, the prospective client may possibly be in need of a consultant. Arrive at your appointment exactly on time, bring extra copies of your resume, and be ready to tell prospective clients how your service can help them.

Follow up your interview with a thank-you letter and a final offer of service.   Even if your interview seemed fruitless, send a follow-up thank-you letter to the individual who took the time to interview you. In addition to thanking the person, offer your services one more time. This letter may be the very piece of paper that brings you an assignment. Your courtesy might be the one reason the client remem-

FIGURE 3. A sample business thank-you letter.

```
                    GEORGE SMITH - CONSULTANT

                        OFFICE INTERIORS
                         4555 Coleman
                    San Francisco, CA 94112
                         415/555-3465


                                            June 3, 198x


    Andrew Brown, President
    BROWN MANUFACTURING
    555 Fleetwood Avenue
    Oakland, CA 95111


    Dear Mr. Brown:

            Thank you again for taking the time to meet with
    me on Tuesday, June 2.  It was a pleasure to talk with you about
    your upcoming projected expansion.  If you have any additional
    questions about my service that may have come up since our meet-
    ing I will be happy to try to answer them.  I can be contacted at
    my home office at the above number, or if you wish I will be glad
    to drop by and see you again.

            I would like to work with you on your new office
    plan and would appreciate being given a chance to make a full
    proposal.

                                    Sincerely,

                                    George Smith
                                    George Smith
```

bers you above other consultants when a contract is to be awarded. Figure 3 is an example of a business thank-you letter.

ONGOING MARKETING PROGRAMS

Once you have an active list of established clients and a growing list of prospective clients, you will need ongoing marketing programs to remain in touch with one group and make contact with the other. Even when you are busy on an assignment you should continue to plan for future needs. When one job is finished, have another lined up to begin. When you have too many idle days between jobs because of sporadic marketing, your overall income decreases.

The following marketing programs are designed to make a dual outreach—to maintain contact with established clients by one method and to acquire a growing number of prospective clients by another method.

An Ongoing Marketing Program
for Established Clients

Former clients who were satisfied with your work are your best source of future assignments for two reasons. These people may retain your services again, or they may recommend your services to others. An enthusiastic recommendation from a satisfied client is the best advertising you can get and it carries twice the authority of anything you can say about yourself. For this reason, keeping in touch with former clients is doubly important. The following threefold marketing program will keep you from being forgotten by former clients.

Keep your phone busy.   Make friendly calls to former clients at regular intervals. Ask about their business and ask to be included in future consulting plans. Once you cease contact with a client you may be forgotten, or your lack of attention may make clients think you are no longer seeking assignments. Call clients. Never count on them calling you. Few will bother.

Make personal visits.   On days when you are not on assignment get out on the street and make personal visits on former clients. These visits should be brief—just long enough to say hello and remind the client that you are available for work. If you have an updated resume your client hasn't seen, leave a copy.

If a client is not in or is unable to see you when you call, leave a personal note on the back of your business card with the date and time of your call. Follow up on notes with phone calls the day after to tell clients you were sorry to have missed seeing them. Again ask for assignments.

Send letters.   Contact can be maintained with former clients through friendly personal letters. These letters should be brief but lighter in tone than a first-contact type of letter. These letters are strictly promotional, and your clients know this; still they need not sound like a paid advertisement. Personal letters might be written for the following reasons:

- to send seasonal greetings or extend congratulations for promotions or new business ventures
- to extend an invitation to a luncheon or a meeting
- to send news of projects similar to those a client is interested in

Figure 4 is an example of a personal promotional letter.

An Ongoing Marketing Program
for Prospective Clients

It is a well-known fact that no client-consultant relationship is eternal. Clients drift away, move away, or go out of business, and you must continually seek new sources for assignments. This book's basic plan, designed to contact prospective clients (described in the beginning of Chapter 3), should be continued on an ongoing basis. Use introductory letters with resume, follow up with phone calls, and make personal visits to bring in new clients.

In addition to this basic program you should try other ways to make contacts with prospective clients. Some of the following suggestions may work for you.

```
                    GEORGE SMITH - CONSULTANT

                       OFFICE INTERIORS
                         4555 Coleman
                    San Francisco, CA 94112
                        415/555-3465


                                        December 15, 198x


    Andrew Brown, President
    BROWN MANUFACTURING
    555 Fleetwood Avenue
    Seattle, Washington 98105


    Dear Mr. Brown:

            Best wishes to you and your fine staff for a
    good holiday season.

            I enjoyed working with you on your new office
    project this past August and hope you are enjoying the
    convenience of your new addition.  If at any time in the
    future I can be of further help I would be pleased to
    receive a call.

            May the coming year bring growth and progress
    to your business.

                              Sincerely,

                              George Smith
                              George Smith
```

FIGURE 4. A personal promotional letter.

Advertise. Not all consultants want to advertise. Once you offer your services to the public at large you lose some control over assignment choice. When you contact a client in person, you select where you want to work. When a client follows up on your advertisement and contacts you, that freedom of choice is eliminated. Of course, you can decline a job offer from someone who answers your advertisement, but too many turndowns may eventually cause hard feelings and may damage your reputation. However, if you can afford to advertise and your prospective client list needs reinforcing, you may want to run short notices in a periodical or publication directed to your profession.

Keep your advertisement copy simple, and avoid sounding self-laudatory. List your services and your phone number, but don't include your address unless you are using a national publication. Printing an address may be paying for words that bring few results. Most clients don't want to bother to write a letter, preferring to contact you by phone. When your advertisement appears in print be ready to answer the phone or you have wasted your money. Few clients will bother to phone a second time if they get no answer on their first call.

Join professional organizations.   Many professions support organizations dedicated to promoting that profession. Join a group in your profession and get to know your colleagues. You may be offered assignment leads by fellow members.

Develop a good reputation.   There are many times you can volunteer to help with community projects that may lead to consulting assignments. When you volunteer your time and talent to help out in a nonprofit organization or with a community project, you begin to be known for that talent. For example, a graphic artist who volunteers to design posters for a community fund-raising event may end up with paying assignments from people who see and like the posters.

Write articles about your profession.   If you have modest communicating skills you may want to write short articles about your profession for local newspapers or trade, technical, and professional journals. Many editors welcome concise and informative pieces. These markets may not pay, except in contributor's copies, but they may bring in clients for your business.

Accept public speaking engagements.   Never turn down an invitation to speak to groups and classes about your profession. Members of your audience could be prospective clients.

In the broad, general scope, offices that come under the heading of government include subdivisions, departments, and agencies of:

- Federal government
- State government
- County government
- Municipal government

These divisions also include:

- Districts and commissions authorized by national, state, county, or municipal law
- Independent and quasi-public governmental authorities

Both long-term and short-term contracts are available for qualified consultants at city, state, and federal government levels, and much of this work can be obtained without grant application. Winning government contracts requires some knowledge of how contracts are offered, some understanding of government structure, a little persistence to find your way through paper work, and a little patience to wait out contract authorization.

To win a government consulting assignment you should do one of two things: Follow up on government-advertised leads, or make contacts with personnel in government division offices and offer them your services.

How Federal Government Contracts Are Advertised

Where government work can be done by regular government employees or, where applicable, Civil Service employees, no consulting contracts are advertised or let. However, federal government contracts that are let can range in size from large projects calling for consulting corporations with teams of consultants to small contracts needing only one private consultant. Usually, the larger the contract the wider the scope of advertising for bids. Government contracts, depending upon size, are advertised in any or all of the following ways.

- *Government grant lists.* Specifications for government grants are published and sent to a regular mailing list of universities, firms, contractors, and private businesses.

- *U.S. Post Office bulletins.* Notices are printed that bids will be taken for large federal grants with a description of the grant. These notices appear in U.S. Post Office bulletins under the authority of the U.S. Department of Commerce. They are circulated to mailing lists of applicants who have submitted requests for their receipt.

- *The* **Commerce Business Daily**. The U.S. Department of Commerce issues a publication called the *Commerce Business Daily*, which lists job specifics, budget allocations, and dates concerning proposed government contract awards.

- *U.S. Department of Commerce field offices.* These offices supply information about government contract awards, including those listed in the *Commerce Business Daily*.

- *Minority Business Development Agency.* Under the U.S. Department of Commerce, the Minority Business Development Agency offers help and information to minority persons in business enterprises. Information about government contracts is included. Individuals need not be minorities to request information from this agency.

- *Informal methods of advertising contracts.* Federal government department heads looking for qualified consultants are no different from any other employer when they are seeking applicants by informal means. Consultants may be sought for government contracts in any or all of the following ways: special notices sent to nonprofit organizations, advertisements in local and professional publications, resumes sent by applicants, other department heads' recommendations, and contacts with consultants known personally.

State, county, and municipal governments seek applicants in a manner very similar to that of the federal government. Special bulletins, publications, and mailing lists are used for contacting qualified persons.

How to Make Contacts to Win
Government Assignments

To win government consulting contracts you should follow up on the government-advertised leads previously discussed or make initial contacts with personnel in government division offices. The following suggestions may help you contact government agents who award the contracts.

Get your name on the Bidder's Mailing List. Write or phone the office of the U.S. Department of Commerce, Department of Procurement, in your area, and ask for an application for the Bidder's Mailing List (Form #129). When you return the application, you will be added to the mailing list. You will receive information concerning proposed procurements, sales, and contract awards relating to your field as you have specified on your returned application.

Contact government contract officers. Since almost all government contracts from any sector of government are issued at the department or the agency level where the specific needs are best known and money has been allocated, this level is where you should start your search for assignments. Look in the white pages of your telephone book under any of the various branches of federal, state, county, and municipal government. Seek out the departments you are qualified to work for and call those departments. Ask for the department contract manager or for the division contract officer. Tell this person you are seeking assignments and briefly list your qualifications. Ask if you may send a resume to be kept on file. For example, a mining engineer might call the State Office of Mines and Geology; a bookkeeping consultant might call the City Controller's office at city hall; and a registered nurse might call the U.S. Government Health and Human Services Department, Office of Child and Family Health.

Visit government departments and agencies. Once you have made telephone calls and have sent your resume to different department heads, you should call in person to introduce yourself to the contract managers. Calls to solicit work should be made on a regular basis, the same as those made to clients in the private business sector.

Contact large consulting firms.   Large government grants awarded to consulting firms may create a need for additional consulting help within the winning firms. Read newspapers to see which corporations have been awarded contracts and follow up with calls to these firms to ask for work to fill in during their peak period.

Advertise in local papers.   Your advertisement in a local paper may be read by a government contract officer looking for a consultant with your background.

Ask people you know who work for the government.   Tell friends and acquaintances in government that you are looking for consulting assignments. These people may just hear of an agency in need of your services.

How to Understand
the Government Approval System

Most steps taken toward contract approvals are made to save funds, double check needs, and assure that the public is getting the best service for the money. Most government approval systems advance along these lines:

1. A government agency or department head with a need for consulting service assigns personnel to an internal search to see if the work can be done by someone already on the staff.
2. If no Civil Service or staff employee is available to do the department work, needed contracts are advertised, proposals are accepted, and a consultant is selected.
3. A contract between authorized personnel in the government agency and the consultant is drawn up and signed.
4. The contract is checked and approved by the agency's legal department.
5. The contract is sent to the chief administrative officer of the division for approval.
6. The contract and specifications are sent to the agency's purchaser for approval.
7. The contract and fee schedule are sent to the department controller to certify that funds are available to honor payment.
8. Work proceeds.

The Benefits of Working
for the Government

Going to work for a government agency has several advantages. For example, the pay is usually good, and expense accounts for travel or other needed outlays are fair. Payment is generally prompt and according to schedule. Also, working conditions are safe and comfortable. Getting a government contract is well worth the effort and not difficult at all once you learn the procedure.

HOW THE ECONOMY
AFFECTS THE CONSULTING MARKET

There are two very divergent schools of thought among consultants concerning the effects of the economy upon the amount of consulting work available on an assignment basis. Some consultants claim a "boom" is good for their business; others contend that a "bust" brings in more assignment calls. Here is the reasoning behind both claims.

How Low Periods in the Economy
Might Hurt Consulting Business

Many consultants contend that their business thrives when the overall economy is good and that *less* work is available for consultants during a time of economic recession. They offer the following reasons:

- Company budgets are slashed, and projects that consultants are traditionally hired to assist with are postponed or cancelled.
- Management puts emphasis on increased productivity among regular employees and a moratorium on hiring outside help.

A poor economy may have another fallout effect on the consulting business besides fewer jobs. Clients who are having trouble meeting their bills are apt to put off paying consultants. The payroll for regular employees is almost always met ahead of the vouchers submitted by consultants.

During times of economic stress consultants should be doubly alert for troubled companies who are slow to pay. Penalty clauses and stop-work clauses should be considered in contracts signed with less than stable clients.

How Low Periods in the Economy Might Help Consulting Business

Some consultants contend that *more* work is available for consultants during a time of economic recession for the following reasons:

- Companies cut back on regular staff by means of attrition or layoffs because regular employees must be paid through both peak and valley workload periods. Consultants are then hired to fill in only when needed.
- Companies realize that funds go further with the use of consultants who need not be given benefits, vacations, or sick leave.

These theories are based on predicting what clients will do. Obviously, since some clients will do one thing and will see the situation one way—and others will do something different and see the situation a different way—the trick is to determine what your prospective clients will do. One way to ascertain this information is to find out what they did during the last slump.

How to Use a Slump to Get an Assignment

When communicating with clients you should not ignore or gloss over an economic slump. Instead, market aggressively, using the slump to your advantage. When seeking an assignment you should stress the money-saving advantages of hiring a consultant. Here are some statements that may help you sell your services during slump periods.

- Budgeted funds go further when using a consultant who is hired only when work is to be done.
- Keeping staff at a minimum cuts down on overhead for large offices. (Many consultants work in their own offices.)
- Consultants never cost company money for benefit programs, vacations, or sick leave.
- You have new problems due to the slump, and you need new answers a consultant can provide.

Statements such as these can sometimes turn an economic slump into an employment advantage for consultants.

HOW TO WRITE A SUCCESSFUL PROPOSAL

A proposal is an offer made by a consultant to gain a client assignment. The secret of writing good proposals that win assignments is to give the impression of being supportive without being domineering. Most clients look for consultants who are knowledgeable and efficient, yet not overbearing. Clients want work taken off their hands, but they don't want any of their power usurped while that work is being done.

What You Need to Know
Before Making a Proposal

Before putting any proposal into words you should get all the facts about the assignment and any extenuating circumstances that might affect the progress of the work. They saying "time is money" is especially true in the consulting profession. Many factors that delay work and interfere with the course of an assignment can add to the cost of doing the job. Ask the following questions before making a final time estimate in your proposal.

Has the assignment previously been attempted? If the client's regular staff or another consultant has been unsuccessful, try to get a look at the rejected work and find out why the client was dissatisfied. The answer may reveal hidden troubles that could delay work. If several attempts to do the same job have failed or been rejected, you may not want to offer a proposal at all. The assignment might be impractical or impossible to complete to the client's satisfaction.

Who will provide the work area? Find out if you are expected to furnish an office or work area or if the client will. Additional expenses such as travel time and office overhead could be involved.

Will you report to a committee or to one person? Large committees that must approve all work may tend to slow progress.

Is travel involved? If you must work a considerable distance from the client's location, you will need extra time for delays in long-distance reporting and approval.

What type of support services will be offered? Will you have to do all research and work supervision yourself or will some workers on the client's staff be assigned to help you? The less help you receive the longer you will need to work at the assignment.

How available will resource people be? If support people have to add the time they give you on top of their regular duties, the project will take considerably more time. Find out where the client's priorities lie—with regular work or with the consulting assignment.

Types of Proposals

The three types of proposals a consultant can offer a client are the verbal agreement, the simple proposal, or the formal proposal. Tailor your proposal according to the circumstances under which it is made and according to the type that your client prefers. For example, a short, simple assignment for a very relaxed client would seldom require a formal proposal.

The verbal agreement.   The verbal agreement, which is nothing more than a conversation between a client and a consultant, is the simplest type of proposal. The conversation would include a discussion of work to be done, length of time needed to complete the work, and fees to be charged. Here is an example of how such a proposal might be made: A client calls a decorator consultant and says, "I want to redo my kitchen. Will you act as a consultant and make suggestions on what should be done?" The decorator consultant looks over the old kitchen and says, "Yes, for $_____ I'll give you two sketches and even recommend materials and workmen." The client says, "All right, draw up a plan and I'll give you a check when you bring me the information."

This kind of proposal may seem desirable because of the ease with which details are settled, but such agreements are actually full of loopholes that could create problems for both the client and the consultant. For example:

- No time limit was set. The consultant might take weeks to do the plans, putting other jobs ahead of the kitchen.
- No monetary limits were set for redoing the kitchen. The consultant might design something far more expensive than the client had in mind.

- No written agreement was made. The client might not like the plans and refuse to pay.

Verbal agreements make poor proposals even between people who know each other well. Too much room is left for misunderstanding. If your client insists that a verbal agreement is sufficient, follow up your conversation with a letter stating what you intend to do and what the client has agreed to pay. This precaution gives the client a chance to ask questions before the proposal is accepted and work begins.

The simple proposal.   The simple proposal is probably the one used by most consultants and preferred by most clients. This is a simple written statement consisting of three clauses. A simple proposal may be submitted on a printed form or typed on the consultant's stationery. The three clauses include the following:

- A definition of the work to be done, including all costs involved.
- The date when work will begin and the length of time needed to complete the assignment.
- The fees to be paid for services rendered.

This proposal is signed by the consultant and sent through the mail or delivered in person to the client. This simple proposal actually differs very little from the letter of agreement sent to a client after a verbal agreement is made.

The formal proposal.   A formal proposal is considerably more detailed in that all aspects of the work are spelled out in full. It closely resembles a final contract and offers the best protection for the client and the consultant. No proposal is legally binding, allowing the consultant to go ahead with the work, until final client approval is given. Most formal proposals include the following information:

- the consultant's name and client's name
- the consultant's recommendations for work to be done
- amounts and types of materials to be used
- resource people assigned to the work

- the date the consultant is available to start work
- the length of time needed to complete the job, plus work-in-progress deadlines.
- the consultant's fees and expenses to be paid
- payment schedule

The information included always varies with the type of consulting work. Figure 5 is an example of a statement of basic clauses in a formal proposal.

What a Proposal Should Not Include

A proposal is not a contract; it is merely an offer to do an assignment in a certain way, for a certain price, and during a certain time period. A good proposal should never include a list of what the consultant will *not* do. Consultants who take a negative approach with their proposals and list the work they will not do, run the risk of turning clients away. Leave negatives unsaid and let the client ask questions about what you will and will not do. Some additional aspects of the job may have to be negotiated and added to the proposal as a condition of being awarded the contract.

Detailed and complicated clauses should not be included in a proposal. No client wants to take time to read long, detailed pages of copy. If you are too wordy you may lose an assignment. Short, simple clauses are usually preferred to lengthy, complicated ones. In addition, if a proposal takes too many paragraphs to spell out what should be short and simple, the client may become wary and begin to look for "fine print."

Also, do not include complicated legal clauses and employment stipulations in a proposal. These belong in a contract.

How to Present Your Proposal

The neater and more organized your proposal, the more efficient and ready for work you're going to appear to prospective clients. How you package your proposal is nearly as important as how it is stated. Proposals should be neatly typed with all sheets stapled together to prevent loss. Your signature and the date of signing should appear at

```
Proposal by:        Andrew Proctor, Consultant
                    Graphic Design
                    3999 Afton Street
                    San Francisco, CA 94121
                    415/555-4632

Submitted to:       James Morgan, President
                    Morgan Manufacturing Co.
                    1980 19th Avenue
                    San Francisco, CA 94113


I hereby submit the following proposal for the cover design for
the MORGAN MANUFACTURING COMPANY Annual Report.

            Specifications as per drawing attached:

            Design to be the original work of consultant.

            Job start:  Five working days after acceptance
                        of proposal.

            Job finish:  Fourteen working days.

            Payment:  The amount of $_____ to be paid to
                      Andrew Proctor within 30 days of
                      completion of design.
```

Signature _Andrew Proctor_

Date submitted _6 / 10 / 8x_

```
Acceptance of Proposal:

            If the above specifications, materials, and fees
            are satisfactory and the proposal is acceptable,
            please notify consultant Andrew Proctor at the
            above number.
```

FIGURE 5. An example of a formal proposal.

the end of your proposal. A cover letter on your business stationery should be included. The cover letter should include the following:

- a statement that your proposal is enclosed
- an offer to answer questions either by phone or at an arranged meeting

- a request for the assignment, telling clients you hope you will have an opportunity to be of service to them
- a statement of appreciation, thanking your clients for their time and for giving you the opportunity to submit a proposal

Getting an Answer to Your Proposal

Some clients are in a great hurry to receive proposals and are notoriously slow about answering them. Although you never want to appear to be pressuring a client, sometimes it is necessary to take certain measures in order to get a contract. Here are some suggestions that may help you get an answer to a proposal.

- If your proposal has been with the client for over one week, phone and offer to answer questions. You may get questions or you may get an answer to your proposal.
- If you are put off with vague excuses when you phone, wait three days and drop in to see the client in person. Ask if a decision has been made.
- If a client is waiting for a committee decision, find out when the committee will meet and phone the client the day after that meeting.
- Insert an acceptance time limit in your proposal.

What to Do First When You Are Awarded a Job

The first thing you should do after you have been told that your bid is accepted is to thank the client and ask to get together to draw up a contract. Some contracts are merely extensions of your proposal. Some companies use form contracts. If you are asked to write a contract, set a date to have a copy ready for the client to see, and get busy.

What to Do When You Lose an Assignment

If you did not win a given assignment and find out that another consultant has been given the job, be careful how you handle this rejection. If you do not accept this defeat graciously, you could ruin your chances of working for the client at another time. Wish the client good luck on the project and thank him or her for giving you the opportunity to make a proposal. Mention that you would be pleased to submit a proposal for any future assignments.

Do not ask a client who won the job. This sounds antagonistic as if you are challenging their judgment and their right to make a choice. Find out from your colleagues who got the assignment and why that proposal was chosen over yours. You can learn a lot from rejected proposals.

4

DOING THE JOB

HOW TO WRITE A FAIR CONTRACT

A consulting contract is a series of checks and balances drawn up as the result of a meeting between a consultant and a client. A fair contract offers equal protection and benefits to both parties. Each party must realize some gain from the agreement, and, conversely, each party should be held to the agreement by penalties imposed for failure to comply.

A simple illustration of a contract point held in balance would be:

$$\begin{array}{cc} \textit{CONSULTANT} & \textit{CLIENT} \\ \textit{(Gives Service)} & \textit{(Pays for Service)} \end{array}$$

No service $\longrightarrow$ No pay

Stop service $\longleftarrow$ Late payment

Read every new contract through completely even if you have worked with the client many times before. A new contract could contain different clauses or new wording in old clauses. Ask questions about what you do not understand, and ask permission to insert clauses that protect your interests.

Most government agencies and corporations send all contracts to their legal departments for approval. Consultants who do not understand the terms of a contract and who have doubts about what they are signing should also seek legal counsel.

Time spent in understanding and refining contract clauses and working out a mutually satisfactory agreement between you and a client is well worth the effort. A sound contract can get a working relationship off to a promising start.

TYPES OF CONTRACTS

Contracts, like proposals, can range from an informal note to a formal document. Usually, the larger the assignment, the more formal the contract you will be asked to sign.

The Simple Contract

A *simple contract* may be no more than an informal proposal signed by both parties. It is often drawn up by retyping the consultant's proposal to spell out work specifications (either in the body of the text or in an appendix), time limits, and fees agreed upon. Some or all of the following clauses are included as well:

- a work guarantee (when applicable)
- a materials guarantee (when applicable)
- the expenses to be paid by client
- the resource materials to be furnished by client
- the resource personnel to be furnished by client
- signatures of both parties with dates

Figure 6 is an example of a simple contract adapted from the formal proposal given in Chapter 3.

FIGURE 6. An example of a simple contract.

AN AGREEMENT between Andrew Proctor, Consultant in Graphic Design, and James Morgan, President, Morgan Manufacturing Co.

As Consultant, I hereby agree to provide the following services for Morgan 'Manufacturing Company, client:

- Complete finished work for the cover design for the Morgan Manufacturing Company Annual Report.

- Design to be according to specifications in Appendix I.

- Job start: One week after acceptance of proposal.

- Job finish: Fourteen working days.

- Payment: $_____ To be paid to Andrew Proctor within 30 days of completion of project.

- Expenses: Andrew Proctor shall be reimbursed for expenses incurred in performance of services, within 30 days time after presentation of invoice to client.

- Client shall furnish the following resource personnel and equipment for performance of duties during the course of this contract: Photocopy
                                   Secretarial
                                   Mail services

Acceptance of Agreement:

Andrew Proctor
Consultant

555- 98 - 4555
Taxpayer Identification Number

Date: 6/10/8x

As Client I hereby agree to the above contract and clauses:

James Morgan, President
Signature and Title

Date: 6 / 10 / 8x

The Formal Contract

Some corporations and government agencies use standard contract forms for consulting agreements. These forms are then adapted for each assignment by adding an appendix to outline services and fees. Some businesses ask their legal departments to write individual contracts for each new consulting assignment, and some clients ask the consultant to draw up a contract.

During your consulting career, it is likely that you will be asked to write or to sign some type of formal contract. For this reason a basic understanding of the formal contract format and protective contract clauses should be part of your working knowledge.

The following is a list of clauses sometimes used in formal contracts. Certainly not all of these clauses are included in every contract.

• *Parties involved.* The opening paragraph of a formal contract should include the names of all parties involved.

• *Starting and completion dates.* The duration of the contract is written here, or the reader is referred to an appendix attached in which hours and dates are outlined. Contracts may state either the beginning and ending dates of an assignment or the number of working days or hours required to do the job, or both, or a maximum of hours within a certain time frame.

• *Services.* The services the consultant agrees to perform for the client should be listed in detail, by specific task and scope, in this section of the contract, or the reader should be referred to an appendix. The client has already expressed his or her work needs and the consultant has already offered specific suggestions to fill these needs, usually at the proposal stage. The services listed in the contract, therefore, have already been agreed upon by both parties.

• *Additional work.* A clause for additional work allows a client to request a contract modification for additions to the services originally listed. Fees for an extension of contract work should be at the same rate as those set forth in the original agreement. When a ceiling has been set for the maximum financial commitment for a given contract, a new and higher ceiling should be set when the contract modification is made. Any contract modification agreements should be confirmed in writing and signed by both parties. A contract may be extended several times to include additional work, provided both parties are willing.

- *Support services.* The number and type of resource personnel to be supplied by the client should be listed here.

- *Work delegation.* The work delegation clause states that permission is granted for the consultant to hire assistants and delegate obligations.

- *Contingencies.* A contingency clause in a contract protects both parties by stating that all agreements are based on the assumption that the consultant will have complete control of services rendered, except in the case of strikes, accidents, or delays beyond the control of the consultant or the client.

- *Termination.* This clause allows either party to terminate services upon giving written notification a predetermined number of days in advance.

- *Employment status.* Businesses that have benefit programs for their employees usually include an employment status clause in their contracts with consultants stating that the latter shall act as independent contractors who are not eligible to participate in any benefit programs or tax-withholding services.

- *Reimbursement.* A fee outline by amount and a payment schedule should be included here, or the reader should be referred to an appendix. The following points should be enumerated: (1) fee per hour or day and overtime fees, or (2) a set fee for the total assignment, (3) a maximum award per contract, and (4) payment schedule.

- *Expenses.* Job-related expenses to be paid by the client are enumerated here.

- *Late payment.* Consultants taking a contract with a client known to be a poor payment risk may want to insert a late payment clause. Stipulation can be made that any invoice not paid within thirty days of the date of billing would be subject to a late payment charge equal to or slightly higher than the local tax rate or the amount of interest earned in a standard savings account.

- *Stop work.* A stop-work clause allows a consultant to discontinue services when fees and penalities due are not paid within a stated, set period of time. This clause is usually not evoked until after a second billing or until sixty days without pay have passed.

• *Confidentiality.* The confidentiality clause states that all information disclosed by a client to a consultant for purposes of work or that coming to the attention of the consultant during the course of such work should be kept strictly confidential.

• *Product ownership.* A clause covering product ownership states that all materials and ideas resulting from a consultant's services shall belong to the client. Such an ownership clause may not be to your best interest, should a client, for example, reject several proposed plans that might be useful for another assignment. Instead of a product ownership clause that benefits only the client, you should try to get a clause that allows rejected plans and ideas to remain the property of the consultant.

• *Advertising.* This clause prohibits the use of the client's name or business name by the consultant for any advertisement or news releases without the written approval of the client. You may list a client on a resume without such approval. However, if you wish to use a client's name for reference, asking the client for permission is customary and courteous.

• *Legal process.* A legal process clause requires that a consultant be legally bound to cooperate with a client in any litigation involving an assignment carried out by the consultant. Should you become involved in client litigation you would be wise to see your own attorney for advice.

• *Applicable law.* The applicable law clause simply states that the contract shall be governed by the laws of the state in which it is written.

• *Signatures.* The closing paragraph of a contract should contain the signatures of both parties included in the agreement and the dates of those signatures. Some clients also ask for a taxpayer identification number from the consultant; this number is used to send the consultant a report of earnings and for tax reporting purposes.

For a contract to be legal, the individual who signs the contract must have the legal authority to do so.

In the example of the formal contract (Figure 7) below and on the following two pages, all the clauses previously mentioned are included. It is not likely, however, than an actual contract would contain every one of these clauses.

Andrew Proctor (hereinafter called "consultant"), by acceptance hereof, agrees to provide the following services to James Morgan, MORGAN MANUFACTURING COMPANY (hereinafter called "client") upon the terms and conditions set forth herein.

Services:

Consultant agrees to perform for client the services listed in the Service Section of Appendix I.

Starting and Completion Dates:

The duration of this contract, with delivery dates for services, will be listed in Appendix II.

Additional Work:

Contract may be modified to add to the tasks and scope of this contract should both parties (consultant and client) be in agreement on the extension. Consultants shall be paid for such action on the same basis as set forth in this contract.

Support Services:

The client shall supply support services in number and type of those listed in Appendix III.

Work Delegation:

All services shall be that of the consultant unless permission to hire assistants and delegate obligations is given in writing.

Contingencies:

All agreements in this contract to be contingent upon free control of service outside of strikes, accidents, or delays beyond the control of the consultant or client.

Termination:

Services under this contract shall terminate fifteen days after consultant's receipt of written notification from client. Consultant may terminate this agreement by providing client with fifteen days written notice.

FIGURE 7. An example of a formal contract.

FIGURE 7—Continued

Employment Status:

Consultant shall act as an independent contractor, not as an employee, and shall not be eligible to participate in any of the client's employee benefit programs.

Late Payment:

Consultant invoices not paid by client within 30 days of date of billing will be subject to ____% late payment charge.

Stop Work:

Consultant shall discontinue work and this contract shall terminate after 60 days of nonpayment, by client, of fees and expenses billed by consultant.

Confidentiality:

Consultant shall treat as confidential and will not disclose any information that comes to the attention of the consultant during the course of this assignment.

Legal Process:

In the event that a subpoena or other legal process in any way concerning information disclosed by the client to the consultant is served upon the consultant, the consultant agrees to notify the client immediately upon receipt of such a subpoena or other legal process and to cooperate with the client, at client's expense, in any lawful effort by the client to contest the legal validity of such a subpoena or other legal process. The provision shall in no way limit the consultant's ability to satisfy any governmentally required disclosure. The obligation in this paragraph survives termination of this contract.

Product Ownership:

Client shall have ownership of all materials and ideas embodied therein resulting from the services of the consultant unless by written agreement rejected proposed plans and ideas remain the property of the consultant.

Advertising:

Consultant shall not use client's name or refer to client directly or indirectly in any advertisement, news release, or release to any publication without receiving client's permission in writing for such use.

Applicable Law:

This contract shall be enforced in accordance with, and performance hereof shall be governed by, the laws of the State of _____.

In witness whereof, the parties hereto have accepted and signed this contract as of the dates shown below:

CONSULTANT

Andrew Proctor
Signature

MORGAN MANUFACTURING COMPANY

James Morgan, President
Signature

Andrew Proctor - Consultant
Typed Name/Title

James Morgan - President
Typed Name/Title

7 / 2 / 8x
Date

7 / 2 / 8x
Date

The accompanying table contains some explanatory notes.

CLAUSE	BENEFIT TO CONSULTANT	BENEFIT TO CLIENT
Parties Involved	Client agrees to hire consultant.	Consultant agrees to perform service.
Starting and Completion Dates	Length of contract cannot be extended without a new agreement.	Services must be finished by completion date.
Services	Additional services cannot be added.	Services listed must be completed.
Support	Client must provide resources listed.	Consultant cannot ask for additional support.

CLAUSE	BENEFIT TO CONSULTANT	BENEFIT TO CLIENT
Work Delegation	Consultant is not required to hire help.	Consultant must perform services personally.
Contingencies	Consultant is not held to contract when free control of service is interrupted.	Client is not required to pay for service that cannot be performed.
Termination	Client must give notice to terminate consultant.	Consultant must give notice to terminate services.
Employment Status	No withdrawals from fees.	Client does not provide benefit programs.
Reimbursement	Consultant's fees and expenses are guaranteed.	Higher fees and additional expenses cannot be charged.
Late Payment	Consultant may assess penalty for late pay.	
Stop Work	Consultant may stop work if not paid.	
Product Ownership	Consultant may claim rejected plans.	Client has exclusive right to designated plans.
Confidentiality		Consultant agrees to keep client information confidential.
Advertising		Consultant may not use client's name for promotion.
Legal Process		During legal process, consultant shall cooperate with client.

ESTABLISHING A FEE SCHEDULE

Fee setting calls for some complex computation and decision making that many consultants find one of the most difficult aspects of their jobs. Some consultants worry that they may set their fees too high and lose clients, whereas others are concerned that they may set their fees too low and be unable to realize a profit. To arrive at a fair price for your services you must first figure in your overhead expenses, the cost of paying your own benefits, and the amount you think you are entitled to make in profits.

In addition to analyzing your own needs and worth, you should also consider the following outside factors before setting a fee schedule: fees charged by colleagues in your profession, fee guidelines published by your professional society, and the general economic condition in the area in which you practice.

Another factor affecting fees are the job costs borne by your clients. If you have to furnish materials and equipment to do a job you have to charge more. If your client furnishes this type of support or an office with backup personnel to help you, then you certainly should charge less.

Most clients will ask you what your fee schedule is and either accept or decline your services in light of your charges. Some clients, however, establish a basic rate they will pay and will not vary from this rate. If it is your policy to work only at an established rate you should decline to work for less.

In addition to establishing a figure for what you are worth, you must also decide how you want to compute your fees. Basic fees may be computed in one of three different ways:

- A lump sum charged for a specific service. For example, a training consultant would charge a lump sum to teach a certain course to a set number of students.
- A fee based on a percentage of a project budget. For example, a consultant who charges a 10% fee on a $10,000 budget would receive $1,000.
- A fee based on time charges computed hourly, daily, weekly, quarterly, or any other time division agreed upon by consultant and client. This is the most commonly used method of computing charges, and it requires the most detailed billing and accounting procedures.

How to Figure an Hourly Rate

Time charges are the most frequently used method of setting fees both by consultants and clients. Time charges are also most commonly divided into hourly increments. How hourly rates are decided upon varies between professionals. Many consultants arrive at a fair sum by computing according to the following method.

First, decide what you are worth per hour compared with others in your profession. You need not charge the same rate as a colleague just because you are in the same profession. You may have more experience and therefore more value than your colleague. Just as all salaries are not equal for the same job, all consultants' fees need not be exactly the same. Use your colleagues' rates merely as a guideline when setting your own fees. However, if you set your fees too far above those of your colleagues you could lose clients.

Next, add the amount you pay out of your own pocket for benefits. Most regular employees are now receiving handsome benefit packages, but consultants must pay for their own health insurance, vacations, workers' compensation, and retirement funds. Your fees should reflect the cost of benefits you must pay for yourself. To figure the cost of benefits for an hourly rate, compute what such benefits cost you by the week and divide this amount by forty.

Also, determine the costs of promotion necessary to win assignments. You can't charge a client directly for making a proposal, but you can add to your hourly rate those expenses incurred making client contacts and preparing proposals. Don't forget to add on the cost of overhead for maintaining an office and depreciation costs for wear on equipment used in your work. If you don't include a percentage for this kind of expense in your fees, you'll end up with a deficit when you pay your bills.

Finally, decide how much profit you want to make over and above your basic hourly fee. Working for yourself, doing your own accounting and billing, taking all the pay risks, and sacrificing job security should entitle you to a certain amount of profit over and above what salaried personnel would receive for the same job. Do, by all means, take a sum for profit, but keep in mind that it is sometimes wise to shave profits to win certain influential clients who might help your business along.

Once you have decided on a per-hour amount for each of the items listed, add these amounts together to compute your total hourly rate. The computation would look like this:

> Basic hourly fee   = $_____
> Benefits per hour   = $_____
> Overhead per hour = $_____
> Profit per hour   = $_____
> _____
> Total rate per hour = $_____

Setting Fees to Keep Up with Inflation

Many consultants find setting fees difficult during times of inflation. Fees must keep up with costs, but some clients resent paying more for service even when a raise is justified. For this reason most consultants find it best to raise the cost of services only once per year. The yearly set rate, however, must be sufficiently high to cover the cost of inflation for twelve months.

A consultant who wishes to adjust fees quarterly and avoid disapproval might explain how quarterly increases, rather than yearly, can actually save a frequent client some money. When fees are raised quarterly, rather than just once in January, only the assignments billed during the last quarter of the year are charged the highest rate.

During times of recession a consultant should be expected to adjust fees downward. A quarterly downward adjustment saves the consultant money, as fees are left at the highest rate for as many weeks as possible.

Fees Vary
in Different Economic Areas

Just as the price of real estate in various parts of the country can be vastly different, the rates paid to consultants are also different. For example, a tax consultant working in downtown Manhattan is paid a higher fee than a consultant working in a small town in Montana. However, before you Montana consultants begin to envy New York consultants, take into consideration that high fees may not always mean big profits. Consultants working out of offices in downtown Manhattan often pay premium prices for office rental and run up sizable bills for daily commuting costs. On the other hand, Montana consultants very likely have much lower overhead costs, so, although they don't make as much money, their cost of doing business is also less.

Consultants who make proposals on assignments far from their regular work area need to know the average rate in the area where they are making the proposal. A Montana consultant who makes a proposal on a New York job should ask New York rates. A consultant who charges much less than the area's going rate is apt to be considered an uninformed amateur and may be turned down on proposals for this reason.

A New York consultant making a proposal on a job in Montana may need to lower fees a bit to win the assignment, but the New Yorker need not lower fees all the way down to local levels. The reasoning behind this suggestion is that out-of-town experts are sometimes looked upon favorably because they do charge higher fees. Some clients have been inclined to think that higher fees mean better skills. However, consultants themselves know that the top dollar doesn't always buy the best talent.

The best policy for setting fees when bidding on a job in an area you are not familiar with is to research local rates for your type of service, and then set fees using these guidelines: If the local rate is higher than you usually charge, raise your fees to meet local schedules; but if the local rate is much lower than you usually charge, lower your fees to within 25% of local schedules. If rates are too low in a new area, you may find there is no profit in making proposals on assignments in that particular locale.

How to Increase Profits
Without Increasing Fees

You can increase your profits in many ways besides raising your fees. Many contract extras are well worth reaching for, since they often put into your pocket money that clients usually don't resent spending nearly as much as paying high fees. Try the methods described below to increase your profits without increasing your fees.

If you are being paid by the hour, never agree to come to a client's office for a portion of a day. Transportation to and from work is your expense, commuting costs are the same whether you collect for one hour of work or eight hours.

Use company cars, supplies, equipment, and space. Whenever possible get the client to furnish tools, space, and extras. Also let the client supply support services. Get the client's permission to use company secretaries, mail rooms, delivery services, graphic artists, photographers, and other support services and personnel.

Charge authorized purchases to company accounts. Many businesses have accounts at supply outlets. Get authorization from your client to use these accounts for assignment needs. Whenever you spend your own money, be sure to keep track of all these out-of-pocket expenses and bill for them promptly.

Get an advance for travel and entertainment expenses. Draw needed funds in advance and pay a client back what you do not use rather than let clients use your money and pay you back.

Get an advance engagement fee. When your proposal is accepted, try to get an advance payment before you begin work. An engagement fee can be deposited and can be collecting interest before you've actually earned the money. For example, ask for an advance: (1) If you must travel to make a proposal; (2) If you must pay for supplies and services to begin work on an assignment; and (3) If your services are in great demand and you need to reserve a block of time for the client.

Set a minimum job length. Because of the cost of making a proposal and billing for completed work, you should set a minimum length of time for a job. For example, some consultants will not bid on a job of less than one week's duration or for a fee less than $2,000.

Charge premium pay for assignments requiring work at odd hours. Clients who ask you to work split shifts, half days, part of each week, or evening hours should be charged higher fees.

Ask for a bonus for meeting certain contract conditions. If you are willing to work a little harder for longer hours to shave costs, you can often earn a bonus for this extra effort. Here are two bonus-earning tactics:

- For a client who is in a great hurry to get a job done, agree to work overtime and come in ahead of scheduled deadlines. The bonus could be a number of dollars for every day you shave off allotted time.
- For a client who needs to save money, agree to complete a job under the amount allocated in the budget. The bonus could be a percentage of the amount you save the client.

Guaranteed Income from Retainer Fees

Working on retainer is a consulting assignment about halfway between regular employment and contract work. A consultant who is on retainer is "on call" on a regular basis for one particular client. Consultants aren't usually asked to serve on retainer until they have worked for a client a number of times and have gained a continuity of knowledge about the client's business.

When there is a continuing need for the services of a consultant for certain periodic duties, the client who hires on retainer has the guarantee that a consultant will be available when needed. For this service a fixed monthly or annual sum is usually agreed upon between the client and the on-call consultant, and a contract is drawn up. Fees are usually based on the number of hours of periodic work required. However, the contract should state that services requested above the agreed-upon level will be paid additional compensation.

An on-call agreement offers a consultant a certain portion of income on a guaranteed basis, but it also restricts the type, number, and timing of other contracts the consultant can take.

How Cash Management
Can Help Fees Grow

Many financial institutions and other money-conscious businesses have a policy of collecting funds due as soon as possible and paying funds owed just before service charges are due to be assessed. Consultants should also practice good cash management by keeping their money invested as long as possible for the purpose of earning a return. Here are three wise money management rules to help your fees grow:

- Keep extra cash in high interest-bearing accounts.
- Keep only a small amount of needed cash in your checking account. (Even interest-bearing accounts don't earn top dollar.)
- If you can't manage your finances, hire help.

BILLING FOR SERVICES

The amount of the fee a consultant charges is not the sole secret of a large bank account. The second most important factor contributing to profit, next to knowing how much to charge clients, is to know how and when to bill. Therefore, an important factor in contract writing is getting a frequent payment schedule agreed upon. Unless your client has set rules about payment schedules for consultants, you should try to arrange to be paid on a bi-weekly basis. The more frequently you are paid the sooner your earned money can be deposited into an interest-bearing account and begin earning more money. Clients who pay infrequently or pay late use your money to tally up interest that you could be collecting.

If your contract allows you to bill bi-weekly, don't lump your bills to save yourself a little effort and collect only once a month. Bill on time and get your money on time.

What Your Bill Should Include

Your bill should be a clear-cut, formal statement addressed to the person authorized to approve payment. (See Figure 8 for a sample consultant's bill.) This is usually the person who was authorized to sign the contract. Wording for your bill should always include the following:

- date bill is mailed
- your name, address, and telephone number typed on your bill if you are not using your consultant's stationery
- the name and address of the person billed
- enumeration of services
- dates services were performed with total hours worked
- total charges for services, with expenses billed separately
- date charges are due and payable
- your signature and a thank you.

You will need three copies of your bill: one original and two carbons or photocopies. The original and one copy should go to your client; one copy should remain in your files.

Delivering Your Bill

Whenever possible, deliver your bills in person. When you personally hand a client your bill, no excuses can be made later that your message was not received.

What to Do about Late Paying Clients

Before signing a contract be sure to investigate a client's payment reliability. A client with poor credit could cost you money. Consider late-payment or stop-work clauses in your contract if you are signing with a new client who has a record of poor payment, or if you are signing with a client who has been slow to pay you in the past. You

```
From:   Bradley L. Murphy                          July 15, 198x
        555 Market Street
        San Francisco, CA 94110
        (415/555-6060)

To:     Arthur Wilmot, Vice-President
        QUILL INSURANCE COMPANY
        89 Ortega
        San Francisco, CA 94255

                    For services rendered:

                            Critique of introductory brochure
                            with report and recommendations.

                    Dates services were performed:

                            July 9 and 10, 198x
                            (Total 16 hours)

                    Charges for services:

                            16 hours @ $50.00 per hour = $800.00

                    Due and payable on or before August 15, 198x

                                    Thank you,

                                    Bradley L. Murphy
```

FIGURE 8. An example of a consultant's bill.

don't do yourself or your client a favor by letting a large bill accumulate. When you collect regularly, your fees seem more reasonable to the client, but if you let a client hold off on payment until you have to present several bills at one time, your fees always seem larger. And sometimes, when you are lax about collecting the payment that is owed to you, your client may spend that money for something else.

Why Payments Are Late

There are four common reasons why payments for consulting services may be late.

1. The client is careless. Some people treat bill paying pretty lightly.
2. A delay is caused by company payment procedures. Computers are blamed for all kinds of things including late payment, but sometimes you need to bear with slight human or mechanical errors or slight corporate delays due to routines.
3. The client habitually and deliberately pays late in order to use consultant's money. When clients hold on to your money you can't be earning interest.
4. The client doesn't have the money. A business that operates on a very thin margin may not always be able to pay when billed.

How to Collect Late Payments

If late payment is caused by occasional carelessness or a snag in corporate payment procedures, take a tactful approach in trying to collect what is due you. Keep your relationship with the client on a friendly basis so that you will be called on to work for this person again in the future. Here are three ways to delicately suggest that payment is overdue without seeming to pressure:

- If you mailed your bill or sent it by messenger, phone the client to ask if your bill was received, even if you are sure it arrived.
- Call on the client in person and ask if the job was satisfactory. If the answer is yes, remind the client that payment for the work is due.
- Bill a second time, but do not add on the late payment charge allowed in your contract.

Use different tactics entirely if payment is late because a client is deliberately stalling in order to keep money owed you in an interest-bearing account, or if the client has ignored your bills in order to make other purchases. You may not want to work with this client in the future anyway, so less subtle pressure can be used when you receive no response to overdue bills. One of the following methods may bring payment:

- Bill a second time and add on the ___% late payment charge allowed in your contract.
- If the bill is still not paid 30 days after your second billing (60 days after the first billing) invoke the stop-work clause in the contract.

- Tell the client you plan to report nonpayment to the Better Business Bureau, and then do so.
- If the debt is large, tell the client you plan to turn the account over to a collection agency, and then do so. You'll have to pay a fee for collection service, based on a percentage of the amount collected, but you may at least get some of the money owed you.

If all attempts to collect on an account fail, record bad debts and report them to your accountant at the end of the year. Uncollectable accounts are deductible on your taxes.

COLLECTING EXPENSES

The difference between profit and loss on an assignment can depend upon how well you keep track of expenses and how diligent you are about collecting those expenses that are repayable. Small out-of-pocket expenses that are continually forgotten can add up to big losses over the years. Keeping an expense record calls for constant vigilance, but this task should be considered one of the necessary aspects of consulting work.

The consultant who forgets to ask for expenses in a contract or forgets to write down expenses due stands to lose more than just money. Clients who see that you are careless about your own personal funds may begin to wonder how carefully you spend your client's money. Frugality is rarely frowned upon; careless handling of funds is.

Two Types of Expense Records

Consultants should keep two different types of expense records: (1) a record of work-related expenses to be reimbursed by the client and (2), a record of work-related expenses to be borne by the consultant and totaled for tax-deduction purposes. These two different types of expense records should be kept entirely separate. Expenses to promote and sustain your business should never be collected from a client. Likewise, expenses collected from a client are not tax deductible.

Keeping a Two-Part Record System

Consultants who record expenses on the backs of envelopes or stuff receipts into side pockets risk loss. Adopt an orderly system for keeping records that is simple and safeguards you from financial loss. One way to keep track of what you spend is to buy a small, blank book. Divide the book into two sections, the front half for expenses to be reimbursed by the client and the second half for expenses to be totaled for tax-deduction purposes. In the back of your small record book place two envelopes. Label one envelope "client receipts," and label the other envelope "tax-deductible items." Throughout your working day record expenses in one section or the other of your book and place receipts in the correct envelope. At the end of each day the two envelopes should be emptied and contents stored in files. Before billing a client for expenses, receipts should be photocopied, put into chronological order, stapled together to prevent loss, and attached to your expense bill. Payment for expenses should be submitted on the same schedule as your billing fee. Keep the copies of receipts sent to a client in your files. However, if you are billing a client for business calls made on your personal phone, keep the original of the bill from the phone company and send the client a copy.

Expenses to Be Borne by a Client

Your contract should contain a clear statement outlining those expenses to be borne by the client. Never put off talking about expenses until work has begun, thinking an agreement can always be made. Don't take for granted that clients understand they will bear certain expenses. For example, you could find yourself paying travel expenses that you thought would be paid by the client and that the client thought were covered by your fees. Consultants usually ask clients to pay the following typical expense items:

- travel expenses other than to and from a local site
- technical assistance needed to complete a job
- special equipment purchased to carry out the assignment and remaining the property of the client
- materials and supplies used to complete the assignment

- miscellaneous expenses needed to complete the work. These could include postage, long-distance phone charges, graphic design, photography, printing.

Ask for reimbursement of expenses that are fair and traditionally borne by a client, but don't get too petty about what you expect clients to pay for or you could lose an assignment. For example, a client shouldn't be asked to pay for your daily lunch except when you are traveling or when you are required to attend a special business luncheon. And sometimes, rather than lose an assignment, a consultant will pay an expense typically borne by a client. Maybe the overall profit on the assignment or the chance to obtain future contracts will outweigh this expense.

When in doubt about whether an item should be a client-reimbursed expense, record the item on a separate sheet of paper and discuss payment with your client. Never bill doubtful items until they have been approved by the client.

What to Put in Your Record Book under Client-Borne Expenses

Always use a separate page in your record book for each new assignment, even when you are working on more than one assignment for

FIGURE 9. Sample record of expenses to be collected from client.

```
Client:        Evelyn Jenner - Bayview Towing

Date:          July 9, 198x


Paid out of pocket:

               National Parking Garage - 3 hours     $7.50
               (New site visit)

               Quick Print Co.                        $8.50
               (Photocopies of job sheets)

Charged to home phone:

               3 calls to Chicago
               (Re: Water pump - Alpha Equipment)
               (Check July phone bill)
```

```
                                        July 15, 198x

From:        Leona Brian, Structural Engineer
             6859 Olly Avenue
             San Mateo, CA 94098
             415/555-6565

To:          Evelyn Jenner, Sr. Vice-President
             BAYVIEW TOWING COMPANY
             7444 Waterway Road
             South San Francisco, CA 94766

                  For work-related expenses:
                  (Receipts attached)

                      July 9, 198x
                  National Parking Garage - 3 hours      $7.50
                  (New site visit)

                  Quick Print Company                    $8.50
                  (Photocopies of job sheets)

                  3 Phone calls Alpha Equipment           $7.06
                  (Re: New water pump)

             Total expenses due to date.................$22.56

             Due and payable on or before August 15, 198x

                            Thank you,

                            Leona Brian
```

FIGURE 10. Sample bill to client for the expenses listed in Figure 9.

the same client. Your records should show the date money was spent, where the money was spent, and for what reason. See Figure 9 for sample entries in the consultant's record book. A sample bill of these client-borne expenses is illustrated in Figure 10.

What to Put in Your Record Book
under Tax-Deductible Expenses

The cost of doing business can be deducted from the profits you earn, thus reducing the amount of income tax you will have to pay as a self-employed person. Figure 11 illustrates sample entries of tax-deductible items in your record book. Here are a few typical expenditures you might rightfully record in your record book as work-related expenses. When in doubt about a tax-deductible item, always consult your accountant.

- the cost of commuting to and from work
- business development expenses such as advertising in professional journals, mailings to prospective clients, and the cost of doing proposals
- office overhead, including typing and answering services, stationery and supplies, and rent
- special publications and memberships relating to your profession
- the cost of special equipment to do your work

```
Date:      Record date money is spent.

Paid out of pocket:

        U.S. Postal Service           $18.00
        (Stamps for promotional mail)

Charged to store account:

        DANFILL PAPER CO.             $64.00
        (Stationery with letterhead)
```

FIGURE 11. Sample record of expenses for tax deduction.

Receipts for postage and stationery should be retained, as well as for all other expenses. These receipts should be batched monthly and kept to show your accountant when your tax report is being prepared. Receipts are part of your permanent tax record. Tax-deductible expenses should be totaled monthly and quarterly. More information about tax records is provided in Chapter 6.

MEETING DEADLINES

The best way to meet a deadline is to start with a realistic goal. Be sensible about dealing with all demands no matter how much clients pressure you to hurry.

Don't be tempted to try to win a proposal by saying you can do a job in four weeks when you know the actual work will take more like six. You may win the proposal with this unrealistic deadline, but when you fail to finish in four weeks you will probably lose that client for future jobs.

From a client's points of view, the less time needed to do a job, the fewer fees needed to pay the consultant. But rush jobs that don't meet all needs are not bargains either.

What You Need to Know
to Set a Deadline

At your first meeting with a client explain that you cannot set a deadline in your proposal until you know all the facts about the scope of the services needed, where the work is to be done, and who will approve progress.

Even after getting all the facts, wait to set a final deadline for project completion until after you have been awarded the assignment and the contract has been signed by all parties. Deadlines can come up fast when signatures are slow in coming.

Another way of setting a deadline for work completion is to state in your proposal that, "barring unforeseen contingencies the work will be completed within _____ working days after the start of the project."

Any or all of the following factors can delay progress on an assignment. Get answers to these queries before setting a deadline and drawing up a timetable:

- Are all materials available?
- Has a final budget been approved and are funds available to pay vendors and other service personnel?
- Has management approved time for resource people who will assist with the project?
- Will any approvals need to come from out-of-town clients?
- Will other consultants be doing parts of the assignment?

How to Draw Up a Project Timetable

One of the first steps of an assignment should be drawing up a project timetable. Start at the completion date of a project and work

April 1.	Proposal accepted, contract signed, finished project deadline set for April 30.
April 3.	Consultant presents timetable and tentative plan.
April 6.	Consultant presents finished room sketches.
April 8.	Client returns plan with all approvals.
April 9.	Work begins.
April 13.	Client visits site.
April 15.	Consultant gives client written progress report.
April 20.	Client visits site.
April 25.	Consultant gives client written progress report.
April 27.	All work completed. Client visits site.
April 28.	Client gives written approval of work.
April 30.	Open House.

FIGURE 12. Timetable for an office opening—Interior Decorator Consultant.

backward. This plan prevents you from arriving halfway through the work with all the time used up.

The following example shows a timetable for an assignment with a fixed completion date where no deadline slippage is possible (see Figures 12 and 13). Final deadline for this assignment, begun on April 1, is April 30, when a new company office will be shown to business clients at an open house reception. A decorator consultant was called in just thirty days in advance of the open house.

How to Break up Approval Log Jams

Even the best organized timetables have a way of falling apart when clients and client committees stall on approvals and cause disastrous delays. Keeping paper moving and approvals coming calls for a combination of diplomacy and persistence on the part of a consultant. Many times just the presence of a timetable to refer to will keep a job moving, but when this doesn't work here are some other suggestions that have been known to break up log jams.

April 1.	Proposal is accepted. Consultant and client sign contract and set April 30 deadline for finish. Discuss client's ideas for work.
April 2.	Consultant draws up tentative working plan and timetable.
April 3.	Consultant presents timetable and tentative plan to client. Suggestions and deletions are made.
April 4.	Consultant contacts vendors to check delivery dates for materials. Does room sketches.
April 6.	Consultant meets with client to show sketches of finished rooms, samples of carpets, draperies, and wall colors.
April 8.	Client returns plan with all final choices marked. Some suggestions for changes and deletions noted.
April 9.	Work begins.
April 13.	Client makes site visit, suggests changes.
April 15.	Progress report is given to client. Note is made that suggested changes have been made.
April 20.	Client makes site visit, additional changes are requested.
April 25.	Progress report is given to client. Changes noted.
April 27.	All work is completed. Client visits site to inspect work and requests slight changes.
April 28.	Work is finished and approved. Consultant receives a bonus for finishing two days before deadline.
April 30.	Open House. Consultant attends to hear visitor comments.
May 1.	Consultant presents itemized bill to client, due and payable within 30 days.

FIGURE 13. Actual timetable as assignment might progress.

- Visit the client in person and ask for immediate approval of pending plans.
- Remind client that delays are causing mounting fees.
- Inform client that if approvals are not sent on time the deadline must be amended.

When you have tried every way you know to get approvals moving and your client still has the plans shelved, you may actually have to amend your deadline. Although a slipping deadline caused by client delay is not your fault, your reputation may suffer, and you may lose out on any promised bonus.

How to Make up Project Delays

Some deadlines are firm and have to be met. For example, shareholders' meetings and annual reports have legally set deadlines. A printer accepting an annual report can't allow a deadline to slip. Time lost on such assignments must be made up.

When you allow a deadline to slip because of your error or because of your negligence, you should work overtime and make every effort to make up lost time at your own cost. When your client delays progress and causes a deadline to slip, you can make several requests of that client to try to regain lost time. Here are three suggestions.

- Ask the client for additional resources and help from regular employees.
- Ask the client to allow some work to be done by outside services.
- Ask the client to allow some work to be delegated to additional hired assistants working in-house.

You may want to think about discontinuing your business relationship with certain clients who are always slow to give approvals but are always demanding about deadlines. The pressure in this kind of agreement is sometimes not worth the fee you receive, nor is the risk to your reputation worth the effort necessary to keep such clients satisfied.

5

SUCCESSFUL CLIENT RELATIONS

MAINTAINING COMMUNICATION

Even when you see your client daily during the course of an assignment and discuss work in progress, certain types of written reports and letters are still of great value to you and your client. Written reports record exact contacts and activities that might otherwise be forgotten. Letters to your client often serve as goodwill ambassadors, reinforcing in writing what you expressed in person. Reports and letters, in order to serve you well, should be written according to a plan that meets specific goals.

Progress Reports

Progress reports are written bulletins issued to a client to report on advances made during the course of an assignment. Progress reports serve several purposes. They provide clients with documented records of how you used the time they will be billed for; they document the actual amount of time that resource people spend on a project; and they provide a running account of how a project is progressing and whether that project is on schedule.

What to include in a progress report. In addition to dates, the names of people contacted, and the amount of time service personnel

FIGURE 14. One-week work progress report of a Training Consultant with a projected activity report for the upcoming week.

```
       WORK PROGRESS REPORT - August 15, 198x through August 19, 198x
                   WILMA M. HATLEY - TRAINING CONSULTANT

 DATE          ACTIVITY                            CONTACT

 8/15 AM/PM    Meeting to determine policy for     Kevin Jones
               branch training                     Carl Wilson
                                                   Brenda Fuller
                                                   Lee Hallberg

 8/16 AM       Site visit to Wilson Ave.           Jim Brennen
               Branch - Program input.             Anne Smith

      PM       Site visit to Thornton Ave.         Cheryl Brewster
               Branch to check facilities
               for training sessions.

 8/17 AM/PM    Revision of outline for
               Business Development Program.

 8/18 AM       Revision of outline for
               Business Development Program.

      PM       Meeting to present revised          Kevin Jones
               outline.                            Carl Wilson
                                                   Brenda Fuller
                                                   Lee Hallberg

 8/19 AM/PM    Scheduling of training sessions
               with branch managers.
                   Wilson Ave. Branch              Jim Brennen
                   Thornton Ave. Branch            Cheryl Brewster
                   Main Branch                     Richard Sells


       PROJECTED ACTIVITY - August 22, 198x through August 26, 198x
                 TRAINING CONSULTANT AND BRANCH MANAGERS

               Branch training - 3 sessions, Wilson Avenue
               Branch training - 3 sessions, Thornton Avenue
               Branch training - 2 sessions, Main Branch
```

and resource people spent on the project, a progress report should include your work activities and the number of hours you spent at each type of activity (see Figure 14). For example, if you spent two days in meetings, your report should reflect this use of your time. Or if you had to spend long hours researching facts that resource people could have furnished in a fraction of the time, clients may learn from your report that better information resources should be provided on future assignments. Progress reports not only keep clients informed; they help educate them as well.

In addition to submitting a report on your appointments, meetings, travel, research time, and report writing, you should include projected activity at the bottom of each progress report. Planned work for the upcoming report period should be summarized briefly. Included in these projections might be travel plans, special meetings, and planned steps toward the completion of the assignment in progress. For example, projected reports serve to remind your clients that you will be away or that they are expected to attend certain meetings or make project site visits.

What not to include in a progress report.   Questions do not belong in progress reports. Questions should be raised in letters. Expense reports also do not belong in progress reports. Expenses are sent separately as bills.

How to gather data for a progress report.   Producing an accurate progress report isn't possible unless you keep some kind of rough daily log of how your hours are spent. If you rely on your memory to supply a chronological list of events for a week at a time, your memory will fail you. Write down what you do each working day before that day is over.

A log need be no more than a scrap of paper with the date at the top and the names of people seen and events that took place jotted down in order each day. If you make a habit of checking your log for accuracy and completion each night as you finish work, you will have a complete report ready to type at the end of a work week.

Figure 15 illustrates a sample log of one day's activities kept by a training development consultant. Putting down the names of people you contact during the course of an assignment helps to establish those names in your memory. Learning names helps you to get along better in any team situation. Names also provide reference in case of later questions.

```
                                        July 8, 198x

        AM

        Checked reference job aids with
        Helen Roberts.                          2 hours

        Meeting with James Mack and Lillian
        Tay to discuss yearly projections.      1 hour

        PM

        Phoned approval committee to confirm
        Wednesday meeting.                       1 hour

        Checked work in progress and made
        changes in job aid plans.               2 hours

        Met with Eric Noble to discuss the
        hiring of additional writers.           1 hour
```

FIGURE 15. Sample activity log of a Training Development Consultant.

The lasting value of progress reports.   Always keep copies of your progress reports and file them with your other work records. In the future they may provide you with the following valuable information:

- a written record of your performance
- names of contacts that may lead to future work
- indications of time needed to do certain tasks to help with writing future timetables

Your progress reports could also serve to keep your name before clients' eyes, since they most likely will consult their project files when planning future assignments.

Work Summary Reports

At the end of an assignment a final progress report, with a summary of all work completed during the period of time under contract, should be submitted. This final report furnishes the client with a capsulized picture of all work performed (see Figure 16). Clients who lose progress reports or do not wish to take time to read through detailed reports can see at a glance the full services performed by the consultant.

WORK SUMMARY REPORT – August 15, 198x through September 9, 198x

WILMA M. HATLEY – TRAINING CONSULTANT

Business Development Training Program

Met with Policy Committee to agree upon
needs for new Business Development Program.

Met with Managers from Thornton and Wilson
Branches to take input for program revision.

Wrote revision of old Business Development
Training Program incorporating branch input.

Program approved by Policy Committee.

Conducted training sessions, using the new
program, in the following branches:

Thornton Avenue	3 sessions
Wilson Avenue	3 sessions
Main	2 sessions
East River	4 sessions
Lane Park	3 sessions

FIGURE 16. Work summary report of a Training Consultant.

Letters

Letters serve many purposes. They back up what you say in person by repeating your words in print. They also serve to stamp the image of your name on a client's mind, and remind a client of your interest long after a phone call may have been forgotten.

Every business letter should have a reason behind it, and this reason should become evident within the first two lines. Business letters written to ask questions, arrange appointments, or furnish information should state their business clearly and concisely with only a brief note of personal regard in closing. Busy clients don't want to have to read a dozen lines of light news to get to the business of a letter. Good business letters promote an image of intelligence and efficiency and should be balanced with a personal feeling of interest and concern for client needs.

Generally speaking, letters written by consultants to clients fall

FIGURE 17. Letter of confirmation.

GEORGE SMITH – CONSULTANT

OFFICE INTERIORS
4555 Coleman
San Francisco, CA 94112
415/555-3465

April 11, 198x

Andrew Brown, President
BROWN MANUFACTURING
555 Fleetwood Avenue
Seattle, Washington 98105

Dear Mr. Brown:

This is to confirm our appointment date of 10:00 A.M. on Tuesday, April 16, at your office.

Should this time prove inconvenient please phone me at the above number and I will be happy to change to another time or date.

I look forward to meeting with you.

Sincerely,

George Smith

George Smith

into two categories—those written to promote good will and increase business and those written to furnish information or get action. Most business letters that fall into the second category are written to confirm a decision, ask a question, or answer a question. Two examples of these letters are found in Figures 17 and 18.

An example of a letter to confirm an appointment with a client is shown in Figure 17. Appointments or any other type of arrangements made over the telephone should be followed with a brief letter of confirmation. This courtesy precludes your arriving at the wrong time or on the wrong day because you or the client failed to note the correct information.

When clients must be contacted by mail to ask or answer questions, special care should be taken to make letters clear and concise. Questions should be stated briefly so that they stand out in a letter and cannot be missed by a reader who only skims mail. Answer letters should include the question asked followed by the answer.

Other ways letters can help you.   Letters can serve as good records in the event of tax questions or any litigation. They can furnish proof that may help you clear up unanswered questions about when you paid your taxes, for instance, or whether you finished an assignment on time, or how many times you had to bill a client before you were paid.

Your letter file is also a good place to look for future assignments. It is like a small history book of your working experience, telling all about your past relationships with clients. Letters reflect both good and troubled times. They remind you of how you got along with a client and whether that client was satisfied with a finished assignment. Cordial associations during past assignments could mean excellent prospects for future work. Reading old mail is a good way to find possible prospective clients.

RELATING

In a recent opinion poll, members of a group of corporate personnel directors were asked what they considered to be the number-one job requirement in today's business world. An overwhelming majority of

```
┌─────────────────────────────────────────────────────────────┐
│                                                               │
│              GEORGE SMITH - CONSULTANT                        │
│                                                               │
│                 OFFICE INTERIORS                              │
│                  4555 Coleman                                 │
│              San Francisco, CA 94112                          │
│                  415/555-3465                                 │
│                                                               │
│                                                               │
│                                    July 14, 198x              │
│                                                               │
│                                                               │
│   Andrew Brown, President                                     │
│   BROWN MANUFACTURING                                         │
│   555 Fleetwood Avenue                                        │
│   Seattle, Washington 98105                                   │
│                                                               │
│                                                               │
│   Dear Mr. Brown:                                             │
│                                                               │
│              In answer to your letter of July 12, I am happy  │
│   to reply in the affirmative to your question concerning     │
│   whether the east wing of the new office will be ready for   │
│   occupancy on July 20.                                       │
│                                                               │
│              All work will be completed by Friday, July 16,   │
│   and the office will be clear of workers and ready for       │
│   occupancy by the close of business on that day.             │
│                                                               │
│              Should you have any other questions I would be   │
│   pleased to hear from you.  I can be reached by phone at the │
│   above number.  Additionally, a complete progress report     │
│   will be mailed to you on July 16.                           │
│                                                               │
│                                    Sincerely,                 │
│                                    George Smith               │
│                                    George Smith               │
│                                                               │
│                                                               │
└─────────────────────────────────────────────────────────────┘
```

FIGURE 18. A sample answer letter.

these executives agreed that *the ability to get along well with others* was of primary importance.

In any type of work, relating well is important, but, for consultants, relating is the key to effective results. Consultants must be easy to work with, fair in their dealings with all contacts, able to fit into many different types of job situations, and most of all able to relate to a wide variety of personalities. When consultants are accepted and liked by the people they work with, the support they receive from these people often contributes significantly to achieving good results.

Relating to Clients

From the first interview until the finish of a job, consultants need to practice good public relations with their clients. Clients are the people who hand out jobs, sign checks, and give word-of-mouth recommendations. The consultant must get along with all types of clients, whether they are easy to please or difficult to deal with, in order to do a satisfactory job and advance in their careers as consultants.

The following pointers are useful in establishing a good working relationship with any client:

- *Learn to listen.* Take notes and ask questions until you understand your client's needs.
- *Promise only what you can do.* Produce more than you promise rather than fall short of projected progress.
- *Don't overlook details.* Survey the whole of an assignment and make time for all requirements.
- *Learn to disagree.* Look out for your client's interests even when your opinions are not popular.
- *Support your client.* Always speak well of the people you work for.

What Causes Dissatisfied Clients?

Disgruntled clients are often uninformed clients. When you fail to discuss fees, schedules, and plans thoroughly, small misunderstandings can grow into major dissatisfactions. Clients can become disillusioned about your services for any number of reasons. For instance, the client might think your fees are higher than they ought to be. Discuss fees at the time you make your proposal. If a client doesn't want to pay what you are asking, don't take the job. Or the client may feel you are taking up too much of the regular employees' time. This can be avoided by stressing the importance of staff support and explaining how resource people can save the client consulting fees. Another problem might be that the client doesn't like the plans that are presented. Present new and different plans until your client accepts one.

Client Dissatisfaction

When consultants are unable to complete an assignment to their client's satisfaction, the consultants are likely to suffer in several ways. First of all, a dissatisfied client can do much to damage a consultant's professional reputation. Also, assignments that have unsatisfactory endings can haunt consultants, leaving them with serious doubts about their abilities.

To prevent dissatisfaction, establish a feeling of understanding with your clients from the outset. Explain your role and function before beginning an assignment, and continue to communicate with your client as work progresses. Follow these guidelines to establish a good working relationship.

- Get early input of information. Obtain all pertinent information during development of your proposal, at the time the contract is drawn up, and at the early planning meetings.
- Encourage two-way communication. Invite clients to speak out when they want changes made during work progress.
- Give frequent progress reports. Give frequent oral reports and, when possible, written reports. Reserve major comments and judgments for written reports.
- Let your client be the first to receive important information. Communicate developments to your client first before information is given to staff members or outsiders.

How to Turn Dissatisfaction Around

If at any point during an assignment your client is not satisfied with the way work is progressing you should make every effort to determine exactly what your client does not like and try to make corrections.

All problems between you and your client should be discussed objectively. Even if a client becomes openly hostile, you should conceal any negative feelings you may have. Arguments are damaging to any relationship and should be avoided when at all possible.

Should you, however, reach a point during an assignment where every attempt to make corrections has been rejected and your client still remains dissatisfied, you may have to ask that client to terminate your contract. Do not take repeat assignments with such a client.

Relating to Other Publics

Consultants who work with and serve many people may have to deal with some or all of the following:

- the client (this might be one person or a committee)
- the regular employees of the client
- job contractors
- manufacturers
- vendors of supplies
- other service professionals, including consultants
- the general public

Form a good working relationship with each of these contacts, from corporate presidents to vendors of supplies, since each one can influence the outcome of your assignment.

Relating to Regular Staff

Very few assignments involve only the client and the consultant working together on a one-to-one basis. Commonly, other members of the client's regular staff work with the consultant on a project. Getting along with this employee team is often basic to achieving good results. Important points to remember in dealing with a client's regular staff include the following:

- *Allay their fears.* Explain your position as a temporary professional who is there to do a special job and not to spy on, or replace, regular staff.
- *Treat all levels of staff with equal courtesy.* Toadying to management while issuing cold commands to staff won't win friends at any level.
- *Learn people's names.* Presidents of companies have names, and mail room employees have names. People like to be recognized by name no matter what they do.
- *Don't make unfair requests.* Remember that resource people may have family responsibilities. Don't ask staff members to work long hours or on weekends.
- *Carry your share of the work load.* Consultants usually have to issue work orders, but they shouldn't be above doing part of the work, too.
- *Stay out of office politics.* Because consultants are outsiders who are often on the job one day and gone the next, they should remain objective in the face of staff differences.

Relating to Outside Contractors

On many jobs, there may be a number of outside suppliers and other professionals serving your client. It is important to the progress of the work and to your own reputation to keep on good terms with contractors, manufacturers, vendors, and other professionals.

Deal fairly with outside suppliers by keeping them well informed of your needs far in advance of deadlines. Don't make unnecessary or unreasonable requests of suppliers, and don't forget to thank them for their assistance. When possible, furnish suppliers with leads to other sources of business. These outside helpers may in turn locate new clients for you as well.

Relating to the General Public

As a consultant, you may be required to give a statement to the press or other media representatives. All material to be released must first be cleared with your client. Get written permission to give a statement or use a quote.

Deal fairly with writers and reporters, giving them whatever information you are free to supply. These people may be in a position to help you with your career some day.

GIVING FREE SERVICE

When asked how much free service they give, most private consultants say "none." However, almost all consultants do some work without pay, and most receive some benefit from this giving. Free service can generally be divided into three categories—work done free of charge (1) to promote business and win assignments, (2) to make up lost time or correct errors, and (3) to help others without thought of self-promotion.

Free Service to Promote Business

Interviews, proposal writing, and contract negotiations are all undertaken by consultants for no fee. These services not only benefit the client, but they are also promotional sessions for the consultant.

Many consultants find it difficult to decide just how far promotional service should be extended and when to start asking for a fee for additional information. On one hand, a consultant who is unwilling to answer questions about work to be done can't win client confidence. On the other hand, a consultant who answers too many questions may give clients enough information to be able to do the work themselves. Here are a few brief guidelines to help you decide how much free service to offer in promoting an assignment.

During client interviews, you should answer questions about your background, experience, and education and supply a resume. You should also supply the names of some other clients you have worked for as references. However, specific questions concerning the particular work a client wants done should lead to an offer by the consultant to submit a proposal.

When asked to make a proposal, consultants should give their qualifications again, briefly define how they would handle the job, outline a fee schedule, and set time limits. A proposal, however, should not include exact details on how a job is to be done. If a proposal is too detailed, someone else might be able to do the job just by reading the information.

During contract negotiations details listed in the proposal should be repeated, but no additional information on *exactly* how a job will be completed should be added until after a contract is signed.

Free Service to Make
Up Lost Time or Correct Errors

If a consultant or anyone hired by a consultant makes an error, then a correction should be made free of charge. In addition, should you inadvertently recommend the use of faulty materials, replacement with better materials should be made at your expense. Should you be responsible for a work stoppage or delay, work time should be made up without charge.

These corrections may cost you your profits on an assignment, but corrections without charge are the only way to salvage your reputation when errors are your fault.

Donated Free Service

Giving free service to charity can benefit you while you are helping others. Donated service adds to your backlog of experience. Additionally, the people you meet while giving your time may some day offer you future paid assignments. Free service, on a limited basis, to nonprofit organizations should probably be in the schedule of every private consultant, even those who are well known.

Free advice to beginning consultants should be one of your professional commitments. After you are established in your field, pass along some of the information you learned by trial and error and some of the tips you were given by other consultants. Some day these same beginners can help others coming up in the profession.

Free advice to friends is expected of you. What writer hasn't had to listen to a neighbor's poem? What dentist hasn't had to hear about a friend's toothache? In the name of friendship, you will undoubtedly give out some free information and advice.

6

HOW TO RUN
A PROFITABLE
BUSINESS

KEEPING OVERHEAD DOWN

The key to keeping overhead down is to do your own work. Consultants beginning on a limited budget should serve as their own management and staff when tasks are to be done. Never pay someone to do those tasks you have the skill and time to do yourself. For example, if you can type, don't pay to have your letters done; if you know how to keep books, don't hire a bookkeeper; and if you have a truck, deliver your own products.

Of course, it is necessary to know where to draw the line on what you can do yourself. For example, if you're not an attorney, don't try to solve your own legal entanglements. Or, if, for instance, you need graphic work done for a report, and you're not an artist, don't ruin a good job with your amateurish drawings. Also, although you should keep your own expense records, it is advisable to hire a tax accountant to prepare your income tax returns.

Three Areas for Cutting Overhead

Basically three areas of expense in every consulting business need watching. These areas are the cost of space, both office and other work areas; the cost of supplies to maintain an office and promote and perform a service; and the cost of hiring someone to do the technical jobs that consultants cannot do for themselves.

Space.   For consultants in every profession an office of some type is almost always a requirement. An office is the center of activity, the headquarters from which messages are sent and received, and, for some consultants, the place where work is actually performed.

Many factors, such as finances, availability of space, distance from clients, and the purpose of the office, enter into a decision concerning what type and size of office you will need and where your working place should be located.

Beginning consultants with limited resources will probably start out working at home. To be satisfactory, a home office should offer adequate, undisturbed space in which to keep files and records. A phone and someone reliable to take messages are also essential. A cluttered area that is shared by other members of your family could result in your records and messages getting mixed up and lost. And when messages get lost, sometimes clients do too. A home office can usually work out when the following conditions are met:

- A private area in the home is available.
- The space will accommodate any equipment, office machines, and fixtures needed.
- The office is not used for client interviews.
- The distance to travel to clients is not too far or time consuming.

A rental office can lend a tone of professionalism to your business that working out of a home office may not offer. And when other reasons, such as distance or use of your office for client meetings, make a home office impractical, rent money for space becomes one of those essentials you will need to figure into the cost of doing business.

There are two ways to save money on office rent. You can rent space in an older, centrally located building in a metropolitan area for less than in a newer, more modern building. Or you can share an office with other consultants or other business professionals who are also trying to cut down on their overhead. Such arrangements can save on rent and other costs such as telephones and secretarial help. However, for this suggestion to be practical, private space for each professional should be available.

Supplies.   Most consultants need two types of supplies—those used to maintain an office and those used to provide a service. Office supplies are usually pretty standard for most professions, but service supplies vary with every type of consulting profession.

Waste of office supplies can add measurably to your yearly overhead. Here are some cost-cutting suggestions that may help you reduce your supply bills.

- Never make more photocopies than you actually need.
- Don't spend money on stationery and stamps to send a local letter if a telephone call will do.
- Don't run up long-distance telephone bills if you can take care of the same business by mail.
- Don't buy new record books every year if you have a thick book that will divide off into several yearly sections.
- Don't purchase new furniture and equipment for your office if you can buy serviceable, less expensive used items.
- Order supplies such as typewriter ribbons, paper, and envelopes in large amounts to get quantity discount prices.

Equipment and supplies needed to deliver service vary with the type of consulting profession. For example, graphic artists need art supplies and a drawing table; field engineers need testing apparatus. Watching waste and buying in bulk can save on almost every type of supply no matter how specialized.

In many areas and in many consulting professions, travel to projects necessitates transportation equipment. For example, some consultants need trucks and trailers for housing a field office. A few consultants who must travel to remote areas have their own aircraft. And consultants who do hydrographic surveys need boats. Here, too, money can be saved when serviceable used vehicles and craft are purchased.

Hired services.   Nearly all consultants need to hire certain services to conduct their consulting business in a professional manner. For example, if you cannot type you need to hire a typist. Even here, however, you may be able to cut down on expense if your typing requirements are light. Hiring the occasional services of a home typist is less expensive than employing a full-time secretary. Other services consultants might need to hire on an occasional basis might include the following:

- accounting, bookkeeping, and tax services
- legal counsel
- computer work
- printing and duplicating
- graphic design and photography
- repair and upkeep of equipment
- research

BUILDING AN EFFICIENT FILING SYSTEM

Files are your personal storehouse of client information that can lead to future assignments. Files can tell you where you worked last year, which clients were prompt to pay, and when those clients might need you again. Files can also tell you what it cost to do business last month or last year. They can remind you when you need to renew a subscription or a license, and they can jog your memory about upcoming seminars and conferences. Files are worth their weight in profits, and, once set up properly, they take little care.

If you want an efficient filing system you need to teach yourself to put receipts, clippings, correspondence, and client notes in the right files each day as you accumulate these pieces of information. Force yourself to do your filing each day, no matter how busy you are, until daily filing becomes an ingrained habit. To help you maintain this routine and make filing easier, place files in a handy location. Filed material should be kept at a convenient height, not on a top closet shelf or under your bed. When you are ready to put papers away files should be within reach.

Most working consultants can benefit from the use of three different types of files: (1) card files, usually kept in a small file box; (2) tickler files, accordion-pleated files with pockets for days of the month or months of the year; and (3) drawer files, legal- or letter-size folders in which material is kept.

Invest in a card file, a tickler file, and file folders when you open your office. Don't let information pile up, or you may never get around to putting papers in order. Until you can afford a file cabinet, you can keep folders standing upright in a cardboard box. As your business grows, invest in a file cabinet with several drawers.

Card Files and Their Use

A small, three-by-five card file with cards containing the names, addresses, and other pertinent information about clients makes a valuable job-search tool. This file keeps client information at your fingertips. You can arrange your file in the following manner: Keep cards filed in alphabetical order with the client's name or the company name at the top of the card. Divide the file into three categories of clients—active clients, prospective clients, and inactive clients.

An *active client card* might contain some of all of the following information:

- Client, or company, name and the name of the supervisor you worked under
- Assignments with client
- Pay rate at time of assignment
- Information about client in other files
- Comments on assignment might include: office and secretary furnished. Pay schedule monthly only. New project scheduled for July.

A *prospective client card* might contain some or all of the following information:

- Name of prospective client or company
- Dates, types of contacts made by letter, phone, or in person, and the types of replies received

- Comments, such as "Client seems interested in service and gives time for appointments, but has no work at present. Keep on three-month call list. (See tickler file.)"

An *inactive client card* might contain the following information:

- Client or company name
- Past assignments with client
- Reason for placing card in inactive file, for example, gone out of business. Moved to another area. Very poor pay record.

Tickler Files and Their Use

Tickler files, with daily or monthly pockets, keep active consultants in touch with their commitments. Tickler files are the best place to keep notes and reminders of prospective jobs coming up, letters to be answered on certain dates, dues or subscription renewal notices, and reminders of times to make client calls.

Many consultants keep both a daily and yearly tickler file. Notes and messages from the month of September, for example, are moved from the twelve-section yearly file into a thirty-section daily file on the last day of August. All material is filed in chronological order. A letter to be answered on the tenth day of the month is put in under that date. Names of clients who may have assignments coming up are filed on dates you have decided to make client contact.

A daily tickler file should be checked each morning for tasks that need doing that day. An active tickler file system keeps moving and renewing itself by the month and by the day.

Folder Files and Their Use

An alphabetized file-folder system helps you to find papers and correspondence in a hurry and can save you both time and money. Letters, receipts, clippings, and reports become the history of your career and the stepping stones to advancement when kept in files where they are available for future reference.

Different types of folders consultants find useful are as follows:

- *Correspondence.* Use a folder for each client and file them in alphabetical order according to the clients' last names. Inside each folder place letters and replies in chronological order, with the most recent letter on top.

- *Assignment search.* Use a folder for each client or prospective client. Keep notes on phone calls, personal contacts, and letters sent.

- *Periodicals and professional journals.* If you keep only one or two copies per year of your professional journals, file these under their titles and in chronological order according to issue, with the last issue on top. If you keep all copies of your professional journals, you may want to use box files for these to save space in your drawer files for less bulky items.

- *Reports.* File reports according to subject matter, with your own reports all in one section.

- *News clippings and articles.* Save articles that relate to your profession, since they can give you leads to new jobs, tell you about new work styles and techniques, and inform you of meetings and forums. Always date clipped articles, note the name of the periodicals from which they came, and file them according to subject matter.

Personal Progress Files

The doctor you visit regularly keeps a file with notations on your weight, blood pressure, and other pertinent health information. One look at this file tells your doctor whether you are gaining or losing weight, whether your blood pressure is normal, and what kind of medication, if any, you took last year.

If you set up a record of your assignment history using a format similar to your doctor's record, you could see at a glance what type of personal progress you are making in your career. Progress information is useful in setting new goals, in keeping you active in client search, and in helping you to see what types of assignments lead to other jobs and better pay.

To set up a personal progress file all you need is a simple form that you can make yourself. Make photocopies of this form for future supply. Figure 19 illustrates how a filled-out form may look.

ASSIGNMENT DATES	CLIENT	HOURLY RATE	COMMENTS
4/1/8x to 4/15/8x (11 days)	A.B. Cline	$45.00	Prompt approvals. Good staff support.
6/8/8x to 6/29/8x (16 days)	Watt Finance	$45.00	Slow approval system. Office furnished.
12/3/8x to 12/9/8x (5 days)	Volmer Co.	Flat fee of $1,800. Equal to $45.00 per hr.	Pay delayed five weeks. Poor staff support.

FIGURE 19. A personal progress form.

INSURING YOUR BUSINESS

Insurance coverage should be one of the first acquisitions consultants consider after they decide to go into business for themselves. To protect a new business against loss, insurance is a must. Fire can destroy equipment and buildings; a lawsuit can wipe out savings; and thieves can make off with supplies. Insurance can't prevent these things from happening, but coverage can help pay for losses when they do occur.

To get the best investment for your insurance dollar, select an insurance advisor you can trust, and depend on that person to advise you fully and fairly. Your insurance will pay you no more than you actually lose, so carrying more insurance than your property is worth is a waste of money. Your insurance advisor will make sure that you are not underinsured or that you are not carrying duplicate coverage and paying for more insurance than you really need. The service of an insurance agent costs you nothing, since the advice comes with the coverage—quite a bargain when you consider that this advice could help save your business in an emergency.

Types of Business Insurance Consultants May Need

Risks vary according to the type of profession; therefore, the types of insurance consultants need will also vary. In this section several different classes of insurance are discussed, but inclusion here does not necessarily mean they are being recommended. You should seek the advice of your trusted insurance advisor before deciding which types of insurance are best suited to your particular needs.

Insurance on vehicles used for business.   If you use a car or truck for business purposes you should carry liability insurance on that vehicle. Liability insurance covers your legal obligation to pay for injuries to other people or for damage to other people's property for which your vehicle is responsible. Liability insurance does not cover *you* or *your* property.

To protect *your* vehicle you need collision insurance for accident coverage and comprehensive insurance to cover the loss of your automobile by fire, theft, or other accidental cause not covered by collision. This type of policy may be written with a deductible clause stating that the insured will pay a specified amount ($100 or $200, for example) of any loss. Deductible policies have lower premiums than those that pay for the entire loss.

Insurance on your business property.   If you maintain an office or a shop where you conduct your consulting business or if you have a large inventory of materials and supplies for your business, you may want to consider several different types of coverage:

- fire insurance on buildings, equipment, furniture, and materials in inventory
- contractors' liability insurance against bodily injury of persons while on your property or while using your equipment elsewhere. (This kind of policy may be written for those who work in many locations.)
- vandalism and malicious mischief insurance on equipment and supplies
- theft or robbery insurance on materials, office equipment, valuable papers, and tools

Professional liability insurance.   Liability insurance safeguards you against personal liability should you fail to carry out an assignment or should some part of your work contain an error or omission. While such coverage is usually too expensive for most individual consultants to carry, many purchase coverage through their professional societies or associations. Two types of insurance policies provide consultants with some form of liability protection. *Errors and omis-*

sions insurance is for consultants who provide a service; it safeguards them against personal liability for mistakes or omission of some part of the work agreed upon in a contract. *Products liability* or *completed operations liability coverage* protects consultants against lawsuit if things they sell hurt or damage someone, or if service they perform is faulty and causes injury or damage.

Personal Insurance

Consultants who depend upon their day-to-day earnings to pay for food and shelter can come up against financial disaster if for some reason they are unable to perform. The following types of coverage protect consultants and their dependents:

- *Salary continuation insurance* pays income to the consultant who is disabled and cannot continue to work.
- *Business interruption insurance* is a form of fire insurance that pays for loss of earnings if a fire prevents a consultant from working.
- *Life insurance coverage* provides a consultant's dependents with a lump sum or payments in the event of the consultant's death.
- *Medical insurance* provides coverage to help pay for doctor's care and hospitalization in case of illness or injury.

Insuring Your Future

Though not a form of insurance, a retirement plan insures that you will have a sum of money put aside for the years when you may no longer be at peak income or when you are no longer able to work. Self-employed consultants accrue no retirement benefits from companies, so they should set up their own plan. Two popular plans, authorized by the U.S. federal government and offered by savings institutions, are the Keogh Plan and the Individual Retirement Account (IRA). Either of these plans allows you to contribute a certain percentage of your income into a special account and defer tax on the contributed amount and interest earned until you are in a lower income bracket at retirement age. Ask your financial advisor for more information on these accounts.

MAINTAINING ACCURATE TAX RECORDS

Every April just before federal income taxes are due, large numbers of people dash about looking for tax forms and begin sorting through papers trying to find receipts. Private consultants need to give their tax reports much more attention than this and over a much longer period of time.

Since private consultants are not employees of any client business but are workers under the status of independent contractors, no tax is withheld from their pay. Consultants need to put aside sufficient savings from their earnings to insure that they will have money to pay their taxes when they are due. Additionally, they need to keep track of expenses, file receipts, and record their earnings. This means that consultants must work at their tax records all year long.

Tax statutes and laws enacted by the U. S. government and by the various state governments are too complicated to provide specific information in this text. Additionally, tax reports from consultants are likely to be as varied as their talents. Therefore, you are encouraged to employ an experienced accountant to help you determine your own personal tax status and liability, and to use the general information provided here as a guide to preparing certain reports for your accountant to work from.

How to Help
Your Accountant Help You

Accountants need you to supply quite a lot of data and information before they can prepare your actual tax report. For example, you will need to determine if you have earned enough to pay taxes. If your net earnings from self-employment and income from other sources are equal to or exceed a legally designated minimum amount, these earnings are subject to federal income taxes. Additionally, in certain states you must pay state income tax as well. You are also responsible for paying self-employment tax, which is Social Security tax for self-employed individuals, unless, in addition to your consulting income, you earned other salaries that took you over the wage base for Social Security. In this case you will have paid the maximum amount due in Social Security tax and will not be subject to self-employment tax.

You will also have to determine whether you are required to pay your taxes quarterly or yearly. When you estimate that your yearly earnings will be over a certain amount, taxes must be paid in quarterly installments on the basis of this estimate. Estimates are sometimes difficult for consultants to make. One year your business may be flourishing, and the next all your clients may have disappeared. You are the only one who can do your income estimate.

You will also have to determine your tax category. Consultants generally practice in one of three categories.

- Sole proprietors, who are taxed on the total net earnings of their business, plus any income from other sources.
- Partners in a partnership, who pay tax on their share of the total net earnings of the partnership, plus any personal income from other sources.
- Stockholders in a corporation, who pay tax on amounts received from the corporation as salary, bonuses, and dividends, plus any personal income from other sources. Any remaining profits after salaries and bonuses are subject to corporate federal income taxes, and, in most states, to income or franchise taxes.

In addition you need to know what your work-related expenses are. This is when your diligence in keeping expense records and receipt files pays off. To determine which of your recorded expenses are actually deductible, the Intenal Revenue Service has provided the following guidelines. To be tax deductible, expenses must be:

- Incurred in connection with your business
- Necessary to develop or maintain your business
- Generally acceptable in your kind of business
- Incurred for nonpermanent items that will not be used for a period longer than one year. Equipment, for example, is not an expense but a depreciable item.

Determine what amounts were paid for depreciable items. Items of furniture, equipment, and tools used for your business should be classed as depreciable assets. A portion of the cost of such an asset may be deducted as depreciation each year of the item's useful life.

When making purchases of depreciable items, keep receipts and canceled checks as proof of amounts paid.

Determine what your actual earnings were. Your record books should show the exact amount. Records should also show if you received checks or cash for your services. Also included as earnings here are bonuses, gifts, prizes, dividends, and interest earned.

Final Responsibility

Your accountant can set up guidelines for you to follow to keep track of your expenses and your earnings. Based on these figures the accountant prepares your tax statement. However, you alone are responsible for the accuracy of your tax statement and for paying the correct amount of tax.

Other Ways Your Accountant Can Help

Accountants practically pay for themselves in helping you start your business. Bookkeeping and tax errors can be costly; having an accountant is an expense that you would do well to build into your overhead. Accountants can help you:

- set up a workable bookkeeping system,
- determine work-related, deductible expenses,
- calculate deductible amounts on depreciable items,
- provide advice on tax planning, resulting in tax savings, and
- file correct tax reports.

WHEN TO CONSIDER EXPANSION

Many individuals decide to go into business as private consultants because they are tired of working for large companies and want the freedom to be their own boss. Some private consultants later decide that working entirely alone is not satisfactory, and so they take a partner or partners, or they go one step further and incorporate their business.

The decision to expand a business may be motivated by a need for capital or a desire to combine with someone who has different technical skills. Whatever reasons lie behind a decision to expand, consultants should research all options for expanding—and the advantages and drawbacks involved in these options—before deciding to discontinue working as sole proprietors.

In some instances the move toward partnership or incorporation can be complicated. The information that follows in this section only summarizes the options available for enlarging a consulting practice and points out the advantages and disadvantages of each. No actual legal advice is intended. Consultants contemplating status change should seek legal counsel to avoid costly errors.

Steps Toward Partnership

When two or more consultants decide to go into partnership to combine their resources and skills and share decisions and responsibilities, they usually draw up a written partnership agreement, affirming what each partner will contribute and how the responsibilities will be shared. A clear statement on how all earnings shall be divided should also be included in this agreement.

Figure 20 illustrates a very simple form of partnership agreement. All the legal requirements have been met, and such a document would be fully binding.

An agreement such as the one shown in Figure 20 could be rewritten, by mutual agreement between both partners, to update goals after they have been met, or to restate the same goals after the two-year period. Agreements that do not list specific goals and that include only a general statement of basic business goals do not need updating.

The second step in resolving a partnership, after an agreement has been signed, is to secure a federal identification number for the business from the Internal Revenue Service. To apply for a number, consultants should request Form SS-4 from their nearest IRS office. If the partnership is to have no employees, this number will act as a tax identification number only, to be used when the partnership income tax return is filed. In addition to the partnership return, individual partners must also file personal income tax returns and pay federal taxes (and local taxes where applicable) on their share of the business profits.

FIGURE 20. A simple partnership agreement.

An agreement between Roy Lambert, Partner, and Helen Wilson, Partner, made this day July 1, 198x and binding until one partner dies or a written agreement between both parties terminates the partnership.

Business Goals: The partnership, a floral design consulting service, will combine the present clients of both partners and market services to additional prospective clients in the full Portland metropolitan area. An attempt will be made to meet the following goals within two years time:

- Two delivery vehicles to be purchased

- Relocation to a new and larger shop on Laman Avenue

- 25% increase in advertisement in local papers

- The hiring of one shop assistant

Contributions by Partners: Both partners to be equal financial backers in equal agreement on amounts to be invested in the business.

Both partners to contribute equal work time to the business, sharing responsibilities and decisions equally.

Profit Sharing: Both partners to share equally in all profits including bonuses, awards, gifts, dividends, and interest earned on investments. Likewise, each partner will share equally in all business commitments, debts, and losses.

Withdrawal of Funds and Payment of Profits: On the tenth day of each month both partners will draw equal paychecks for their work for the preceding month. Amount to be agreed upon mutually, and adjusted upward or downward according to the profitability of the business.

Profits, over and above agreed upon pay, will be shared equally by both partners, or reinvested in the business by mutual agreement. Both partners to have equal financial and legal powers.

Signed in agreement: (7/10/198x)   Witnessed by: (7/10/198x)

Roy Lambert

Helen Wilson

Mary Phillips

Dan Jones

The Advantages of a Partnership

While the task of setting up a multiple-ownership business may seem a bit complicated, partnerships do have several advantages. For example, partners can:

- Share knowledge and skills when making decisions and working out problems.
- Buy more and better equipment and machines by combining purchasing power.
- Share an office and combine the use of hired outside services.
- Increase the number of possible client contacts.

The Disadvantages of a Partnership

Partners can help each other in many ways, but partners can hinder and restrict each other as well. Partners, for example, are legally responsible for each other's actions and debts. When one consultant in a partnership fails to finish some part of an assignment or makes a wrong estimate on a bid, all partners must pay for these errors, in cash as well as damage to their reputation. Some of the principal drawbacks of going into partnership include the following:

- Each individual partner is responsible for the errors and omissions of all partners.
- Every partner is personally liable for all debts, both business and personal, of all partners.
- All partners, or a majority of the partners, must agree upon major decisions, thereby sometimes delaying answers to clients.
- Accounting and bookkeeping become more complicated as each individual partner must keep track of expenses incurred, contributions made to the partnership, and all withdrawals of funds.

Insurance coverage can decrease the financial hazard arising from errors or omissions made by a partner, but some of the other disadvantages remain. The best insurance when taking on a partner is to know that person well.

Steps Toward Incorporating

Incorporating is another way of enlarging your consulting practice. Forming a corporation is one alternative to forming a partnership. Many people avoid incorporating because they visualize corporations as very large, cold, business-like companies. But corporations can be small, informal businesses, too.

Technically speaking, a corporation is a body authorized by law with certain powers to transact business. Basically, the main difference between a partnership and a corporation lies in how tax is computed and how legal liability is handled.

The first step toward becoming a corporation is to draw up a certificate of incorporation. This certificate should include the proposed name of the corporation, the purpose of the corporation, the names and addresses of those persons incorporating, the location of the place of business, names of the subscribers, and the type and amount of capital stock to be issued. All corporations must have some stated capital at the time of incorporation, and this amount should also be included in the certificate.

Since corporations are licensed by the state, the certificate of incorporation is filed with the office of the secretary of state in the state of the business location. All fees are paid to that office. Incorporation laws vary from state to state; consultants considering incorporation are well advised to seek legal advice, though some do make a study of the incorporating laws and see the process through themselves.

In addition to filing a certificate and paying a fee, in some states you must reserve a name for your corporation and have that name approved, file the names of the elected officers, and receive permission to issue stock.

The Advantages of Incorporating

Though incorporating seems much more complicated than forming a partnership, some of the advantages of becoming a corporate business include the following:

- Corporate stockholders have no individual or personal liability for debts or obligations incurred by the corporation.

- Corporate stockholders can become employees of the corporation and receive wages and company-paid fringe benefits.
- Corporate stockholders pay tax only on wages, benefits, and net earnings paid out as dividends.
- Earnings of the corporation may be retained and reinvested in the company.

The Disadvantages of Incorporating

Keeping up with rules and regulations is one of the main disadvantages of incorporating. Your corporation must have stockholders who elect directors, who in turn appoint officers, who in turn hire employees. You must hold shareholders meetings and keep minutes of such meetings.

However, for many private consultants probably the greatest drawback to expanding their business is the sense of having lost some of the freedom of their former status.

CONCLUSION

THE FUTURE OF CONSULTING

Senior marketing executives of two of the largest consulting firms in the United States recently predicted that in the years just ahead the role of the consultant, both corporate and private, will become better understood and that this recognition will lead to increased use of consulting services by both government and industry. Several factors will bring about this growing acceptance of consulting services and the better understanding of the nature and purpose of consulting.

Present clients who are satisfied with the work of consultants will hire their services with greater frequency and will recommend their use to other businesses.

Regular employees of clients will gain a better understanding of the consultant's role, and as they gain more experience working with consultants, they will come to feel less threatened by the hiring of short-term, contract personnel. This better understanding by employees will lead to greater cooperation in support of consultants and result in increased efficiency and productivity by both.

Consultants themselves will act as educators, explaining their roles in business to beginning consultants, to the business community, and to the general public. The benefits to be gained by the use of consulting services will gain wide acceptance as consultants themselves take on this task.

A greater number of private and public educational institutions will increase their recognition of the consulting profession and will offer seminars and special courses on different aspects of consulting. Formal training will lead to better consulting services and an improved reputation for the profession as a whole.

An increased number of books and articles dealing with special consulting professions will be published to augment what is already in print. Also, more professional consulting societies will be formed as consultants from every profession begin joining or forming special organizations to promote and maintain high standards of service. These organizations will publish bulletins and newsletters to advance a better understanding of their services. Members of these societies will also encourage other individuals to enter the profession.

INDEX

Personality test, 11-16
Personal progress files, 129-30
Personal promotional letters, 58, 59
Personal visits, 52, 55-58
Personal work problems, 44-45
Phone calls, 52, 55, 57
Planning assignment, 33
Post Office bulletins, 62
Private consulting:
    advantages of, 40-42
    billing, 92-96
    client relations (*see* Client relations)
    compared to free-lancing, 4
    competitors, 37-40
    contracts (*see* Contracts)
    deadlines, 100-104
    definition of, 3
    economy and, 65-67
    education for, 16-18
    ethics and, 20-24
    expenses, 37, 81, 96-100, 134
    experience in, 18-20
    fee schedules (*see* Fee schedules)
    filing system, 126-29
    financial backing, 24-28
    future of, 143-44
    incorporation, 139-40
    insurance, 130-32, 138
    need for, 4-5
    overhead, 123-26
    partnership, 134, 136-38
    personality test, 11-16
    problems and drawbacks of, 42-45
    specific services of, 32-35
    talents for, 10-11
    tax records, 133-35
    temperament for, 11
    winning assignments (*see* Assignments, winning)
Problems and drawbacks of private consulting, 42-45
Procurement assignment, 32
Product ownership, 82, 84, 86
Products liability or completed operations liability coverage, 132
Professional associations, 20, 40, 60
Professional courtesy, 36
Professional liability insurance, 131-32
Profits, 85, 88, 90-91
Progress reports, 107-10
Project timetable, 101-2
Proposals, 67-73, 119
    answering, 72
    formal, 69-70
    presentation of, 70-72
    simple, 69

verbal agreement, 68-69
Public funding, 27-28
Public speaking engagements, 60

Recommendations, 37
Recruitment assignment, 32-33
Relating, 113-18
Reputation, 60
Resumes, 50-51
Retainer fees, 91-92
Retirement, 19
Retirement plan, 132

Salary continuation insurance, 132
Savings, 26
Selection of consultant, 36
Self-confidence, 11, 12-13
Self-employment tax, 133-34
Services listed in contract, 80, 83, 86
Simple contracts, 78-79
Simple proposals, 69
Sincerity, 11
Small Business Administration, 27
Small consulting firms, 38
Social Security, 133-34
Sole proprietorship, 134
Specialists, 34, 38
Starting date, 80, 83, 86
Stockholders, 134, 139-40
Stop-work clause, 66, 81-82, 84, 86, 93, 95
Supplies and equipment, 36, 125-26
Support services, 81, 83, 86
Survey assignment, 33

Talents of private consultants, 10-11
Tax-deductible expenses, 99-100, 134
Tax records, 133-35
Telephone calls, 52, 55, 57
Temperament of private consultants, 11
Termination clause, 81, 83, 86
Testing assignment, 33
Thank-you letters, 55-56
Tickler files, 127, 128
Trade papers, 52
Training assignment, 33
Travel expenses, 97
Turndowns, 60

Understanding, 11, 13-14

Verbal agreement, 68-69

Wasserman, Paul, 38
Work delegation clause, 81, 83, 86
Work summary reports, 111